YOU ARE THE ONE YOU'RE LOOKING FOR:
Freedom From the Relationship Drama to an
Empowered New YOU!

Published 2009

ISBN 978-1449565824
Published in the United States of America by
W.I.S.E. Publishing

Additional copies of this book can be purchased at
http://www.createspace.com/3406369
and
www.findyourself1st.com

1

YOU ARE THE ONE YOU'RE LOOKING FOR:
Freedom From the Relationship Drama to an
Empowered New YOU!

CONTENTS

INTRODUCTION   WOMAN ... THE FINEST CREATION

Chapter Four   THE FEMININE MYSTIQUE
  - Woman - A Work of Art
  - The Essence of YOU
  - Develop Your Personal Style
  - Upscale Your Image
  - Poised, Polished & On-Point
  - Confidence – the new sex appeal
  - Use Your Secret Weapon

Chapter Five   THE JOY OF SELF-DISCOVERY

  - Who Am I? Exercise
  - Conquer the Enemies Within
  - Tune Into your Transformation
  - 7 Signs of Self-Sabotage
  - Comfort Zone Poem

Chapter Six   CREATE THE LIFE YOU REALLY WANT?
  - Watch the Dream Killers
  - Seek the Power of Intention
  - Wise Women Win
  - You Are a Co-Creator with God

Chapter Seven   MAXIMUM IMPACT – Ascending From Ordinary to Extraordinary
  - Do You Need and Image Overhaul
  - Maximize Your Game
  - You Are A Designer Original - Unique and Special
  - The Attraction Principle
  - Your Personal Value System
  - Your Personal Mission Statement

Introduction

_____

*T*he peaceful sun-drenched street of suburban Chicago was a sharp contrast to the turmoil in Phoenix's heart as she watched the moving van roll away with her possessions. "Well another marriage goes bust" she signed as she glanced at her now ex-husband's house while climbing into her car to follow the truck. "This will never happen to me again", she vowed. "There will be no more anger, deceit, jealousy and rejection from someone who promised to cherish her until 'death do us part'!"

She was astonished that she had chosen wrong for the third time! You'd think that at her age and after all the experiences of two failed marriages that she would know better. "Obviously I didn't learn a thing from that drama", she thought to herself. Once again she had given away all she *had, including her independence, her dreams, her dignity and her heart, for false security and 'in the name of love'. Now she was starting from scratch all over again.*

It was time to gather up all the little pieces of herself that she'd lost and for once in her life become whole. And like her namesake, rise from the ashes like a phoenix!

It's from this place that **YOU ARE THE ONE YOU'RE LOOKING FOR: Freedom From The Relationship Drama** begins.

WOMAN, THE FINEST CREATION

Let's just tell the truth from the beginning. **Women were designed to love men and we were created for relationships**.

So for the primary purpose of being loved by the male, God *made* the female. However, it was not God's plan for woman to lose herself in the process. And God equipped *every* woman with her own individual gifts and personalized purpose to match up with a *specific* man. This means that a woman should not be the one 'looking' for her prince charming, because *not just any man will do.* She should let God do the picking. Remember, God caused Adam to go into a deep sleep while He created Eve so that Eve would be a complete and finished work, nothing missing, nothing broken. God is going to complete His work in you before He wakes up the man He has for you.

In the Beginning, woman was designed to be a 'help mate'. This doesn't mean that she becomes a slave to a man – it means that man needs help! (Even though Adam didn't know it then and most men don't know it now) Consider this. God knew that it was "not good" for man to be alone – because man does not do well without a woman.

God's greatest creation was Adam and Eve in the garden. Woman was taken out of the rib of the man to be his soul mate, to help him be all that he could be and to walk with him, side by side, forever. What an awesome purpose!

But something else happened in the garden that many don't understand…especially women. When the serpent came into the garden and deceived Eve into being disobedient to God, not only did she fall for his guile, *"God knows that your eyes will be opened when you eat it. You will become just like God, knowing everything, both good and evil.*" But she misused her God-given *influence* and convinced Adam, who was supposed to be in charge, to disobey also!

The effect of this disobedience became devastating to mankind in general, and to the relationships of men and women specifically. *Then God said to the woman, "You will bear children with intense pain and suffering. And your desire will be for your husband, he will be your master."* In other words, now woman's Divine *desire* in her heart for man would be changed into a *need* for him…an exaggerated need to get a man, have a man and keep a man, to make her feel loved, desirable, worthy and fulfilled. This is something that no human man on earth has the real ability to do.

9

Now woman would constantly struggle to gain man's love, and her longing for him would rule over her and influence all of her decisions about herself and her life.

Then there's the woman who settles for unhappy relationships because she has decided that any man is better than no man at all. The book of Isaiah in the Bible predicts that *seven women will fight over each man and say, "Let us all marry you! We will provide our own food and clothing. Only let us be called by your name so we won't be mocked as old maids."* The curse from the garden was working then and it is still alive and well today.

Its time for the woman without a man to stop confusing being single with being alone. Singleness means being <u>all one,</u> whole, unique and separate. **You can spend so much time**

looking for who you want that you have no time to be who you are. When you get to the point that you do not need another human for your life to be whole, unique and separate, then you will be ready for the perfect mate you seek.

This book is not about 'hating' on men. Where would we be without a man to Love? This book is about helping us women acknowledge our own personal power and to use it as an asset to project our God-given purpose to attract partners who appreciate it and reflect it.

Life is not fiction and neither is this book. You will meet yourself in this book in short vignettes, through *Meredith*, (who doesn't understand who she really is...) *Eunice* (who's worked herself into a box she can't get out of) *and Roberta*, (a lady-in-waiting). *Candace* (who will give up all dignity to have a man in her life), and *Elise* (who learns a valuable lesson about the 'needs chain'). As well as *Desiree, Renee and Yolanda* (who examine their feminine mystique).

Hopefully, every woman who reads this book will begin to identify her gifts and purpose, so she will know which man is right for her, and begin a process of self-discovery and rediscover the art and power of her own femininity.

The way a woman treats herself sends a message about her goals, ambitions and destinations and about whom she will attract and how she expects to be treated. But – and this is a BIG but – It all begins with us – not men.

I pray that this book will help a woman to develop the savvy to attract a man who thinks the world of her because she thinks the world of herself. Woman, find the perfection in yourself! In short, YOU ARE THE ONE YOU'RE LOOKING FOR.

We must raise ourselves to the level of Energy where we are the light we seek, where we are the happiness we desire, where we are the love we feel is missing, where we are the unlimited abundance we crave.

Dr. Wayne Dyer, Author
The Power of Intention

###

Chapter One

Who Do You Think You Are?

"Until you make the unconscious conscious, it will direct your life and you will call it fate"
– Carl Jung
"A dreamless sleep is death"
– Professor Warren Bonnie

Meredith did the worst thing a woman could do. She settled. Not only did she settle, she lowered her standards to the bottom of the bottom. She could kick herself for doing it again. You'd think that after the last time...and all that bragging she had done too, about having no intention of *getting involved with _any_ man. She could hear herself now.*

"I'm no longer in the business of picking and choosing a man in my life. I'm leaving that strictly up to God! I've chosen wrong one time too many, I obviously don't know how to do it." "Yeah Girl, I'm relinquishing that chore to God – getting' my flawed self out of the way!" Then Michael comes along and what does she do? She settled for a man with a chronic unemployment problem, a secret alcoholic problem, a penchant for womanizing and a prison record for theft! Oh, he had told her about all these things – said he was a changed man that he had "found the Lord". Not only did she brazenly assume that Michael had been sent *by God because he could quote a scripture or two, but then she jumped in the driver's seat, put on her best pair of rose colored glasses...and she SETTLED!*

Meredith messed up in three ways:

#1 - She did not allow her human spirit to line up with her Divine self, by acknowledging her own brilliance.

#2 – She allowed her past to dictate her actions of which the basis was fear of failure.

#3 – Her lack of personal development did not allow her to feel good enough about herself to "raise the bar" on who she would allow in her life.

Sixty-five percent of African American women are single. Many of us say we want to be in a love relationship that will lead to marriage. That's a good thought. But we must also line up our life's activities as well as our personal lives, to be ready to receive that relationship when it comes.

Many women wander vaguely through life looking for fulfillment and significance. Unfortunately, we look for that significance outside of ourselves *before* we have sought the *personal development* needed to get what we want out of life that will attract the ideal mate to share that life with. We go into a relationship looking for love, not realizing that we must bring love with us.

UNDERSTAND THE PURPOSE AND POWER OF WOMAN

Woman is a God-idea. Adam was fumbling around in the bushes, naming animals and God said, "This is not good, this man needs some help! Adam hadn't even envisioned the woman, but God already had woman in mind when He decided, *"It is not good for man to be alone. I will make a companion who will help him"*.

Now the operative word here is "make". The biblical story goes that man was <u>formed</u> of the dust of the earth. If you look at the real meaning of the word <u>formed</u>, it means to mold as a potter molds clay. However, God <u>made</u> the woman, which literally means to "build or construct".

When something is built or constructed, there are certain components that are added for a sturdy foundation. The ingredients of **intuition, influence, femininity** and **compassion** are components God used as the foundation of woman which provides her strength and power. Whether or not you acknowledge that strength and power will determine who you are and who you are to become.

As a woman in today's world, you have to learn to take advantage of the distinct characteristics and uniqueness that you are. Now that it has been pointed out to you how unique and special you are, you MUST believe it!

A woman's **intuition** causes her to have direct perception of truth, to have immediate understanding, and a keen and quick insight. However, trusting and believing that your intuition will not fail you is difficult, because it means you must be totally devoted to your self-development.

To have **influence** produces effects on the actions, behavior and opinions of others and provides an opportunity to exercise a woman's power of persuasion. An accurate example of this is in the Garden of Eden. Eve used her influence to get Adam to eat the golden apple offered by the serpent and create the basis for an entire people to fall into disfavor with God and the lower levels of earthly existence.

The courtesans[1] around the world are masters of using their God-given **femininity** to their advantage. They find fulfillment in listening to their hearts and bringing light and happiness into the lives of men. There is more about this in a later chapter.

The built-in **compassion** a woman possesses causes her to have a deep awareness of and sympathy for another's pain that carries with it a strong desire to alleviate the suffering. The need to nurture others is built into the DNA of woman and embraces all the things that make her feel all female.

[1]A high-class prostitute or mistress in the mid 16th century, usually associated with high class, wealthy men. A famous courtesan was Madame Pompadour, mistress to King Louis XV of France.

How to find your purpose in life and make your life fulfilling? Be delighted with who you really are, you'll have the desires of your heart. In other words, by feeding your inner Spirit, you open up a continual pipeline of counsel, instruction and guidance to lead you to your Divine destiny. When you do that, you will never have to feel an emptiness or lack of purpose again.

KEEP YOUR PERSONAL POWER!

Personal power – it's not aggressive, arrogant, manipulative or dictatorial power, but an inner power that comes from knowing you have all the resources you need to handle whatever happens in your life.

Personal power comes from within and depends upon you approving of you.

When you know your power, you attract people into your life that bring more than they take, in terms of your emotional well being, your self-development and your personal growth.

Women must come to understand that they lose their personal power when they fail to take responsibility for themselves and put all their hopes and dreams into someone else. As long as a part of herself continues to believe that prince charming will come along and rescue her from mediocrity while she exchanges personal accountability and growth for being protected and provided for, she will not maximize their potential for living her best life.

Women have been given a special gift – a Divine power proceeding directly from God...to have control over our bodies, our minds and our environments to be fruitful and to multiply. Now being fruitful is not about having a lot of babies. It's about being **creative**, being **productive**, and possessing the qualities or **power to produce** in abundance, and of **being resourceful** (capable of devising ways and means of accomplishing whatever we set out to accomplish).

Everything we women have - our talents, gifts, expertise, experience and education (self-taught or formal), was put in us to fulfill the Divine vision for us in this earth.

You can't imagine the power you will have when you understand the Spirit that is inside you

Taping into this source within you is where your true power lies. Most women have a very poor understanding of the process that enables them to use and assert their power. When she learns to draw her power from the inside, it helps to alleviate the instability in her life caused by drawing false power from the outside such as what she sees and hears and what she goes through in her relationships, her finances and in her lifestyle.

What is Power? First, I'll tell you what it isn't. It is never control over anyone. People who have the need to lord it over others, only confirms their insecurity. **Real power is your deepest sense of inner peace, your solace in knowing who you are and what you deserve.** For women to get power, we must create it for ourselves. We can't buy it, borrow it, or steal it and the men who have it will not give it to us. Why should they? Power is fun. It's addictive.

We women often give our power away to just to protect ourselves from loneliness, instead of using our power to recognize our deep-seated feelings and desires and to yield ourselves towards using the female components we noted earlier….**Intuition, influence, femininity** and **compassion.**

Giving up her personal power causes a woman to enter into *uncommitted relationships*. In other words, her hunger for intimacy, companionship and a little romance causes some women to exchange their bodies, self esteem, self-actualization and self-confidence for unsatisfying and lukewarm relationships "in the name of love".

Hungry women take whatever and whoever comes along. They are starved for approval, security, intimacy and safeness from wherever they think they can get it. In short, they settle. Why do we do that? Because we often have a frail sense of self worth and a poor understanding of our value. **It becomes more meaningful to please others than to please ourselves.**

We all know women who go broke trying to keep up with the current clothing trends *and* the Joneses. Since they are more concerned with whether they are popular or whether others want to be with them, they are not discerning with their time or their treasure. Often, all any man has to do is show up and he can have whatever he wants, whenever he wants it. This of course bankrupts her self-respect, intimacy and dignity and she's left feeling barren and alone...and of course, still hungry.

When you give up your power, you actually put yourself in a whole different emotional state, because feeling powerful is an emotion in itself.

There are **10 basic emotions** that come into play when you exercise your power:

    1) Love and warmth - all communication is either a loving response, or a cry for help.

    2) Appreciation and Gratitude – when you wake up daily with a feeling of gratitude, you begin to attract to you things to make you continue to have this feeling.

    3) Curiosity - If you want to cure boredom be curious. If you're curious, nothing is a chore.

    4) Excitement and passion – passion is what drives your dreams.

    5) Determination – makes your dreams come to pass.

    6)   **Flexibility** - the ability to change your approach when necessary.

7) Confidence - knowing who you are and *whose*

you are.

8) Cheerfulness - you can choose to look at the glass as

being half empty or half full... it's your choice.

9) Vitality - this can only add to your sex appeal.

10) Contribution – when you feel you are making a

contribution to your world and/or to others, you are indeed

powerful.

AS A WOMAN THINKS...

A spiritual principle and a universal law is that if you

just take control of your thoughts and think the thoughts you

need to think you would be totally transformed. Look around

you. Everything you see began with a thought. Our thoughts

today determine who we will be tomorrow. In other words, the

way you think determines the way you act .

Character is developed through our thoughts and behavior, which greatly impacts our decisions, which in turn determines our level of success. The mind therefore acts as the steering wheel for success. Everything you see in the visible world produces a corresponding picture in your mind. Keeping the thought of the TRUTH is the only way to prevent this.

Statistical reports abound that women born between 1963 and 1970 may never marry. When you hear these reports, corresponding thoughts are produced in your mind, unless you hold on to the truth that you can attract and marry the man of your dreams. When you learn to retain your vision, stick to your purpose and maintain your faith and gratitude, you help to alleviate the power of the faulty beliefs you may have been carrying around all of your life.

GETTING TO KNOW YOU...

Quiet as it's kept, the thoughts we have developed through the years about ourselves have a lot to do with where each of us is in life right now. In other words, the reality you live in right now is nothing more than where your attention lies. Whatever you give your attention to, what you look at, what you hear, the people you associate with, all lead to a well of information from which we draw our thoughts.

Therefore, how you think and feel about yourself is going to be projected in the way you behave. You see, most of the negative tendencies you portray have been acquired through prior action, words and behavior.

Wherever your thoughts tend to travel, on a habitual basis, determines what you do, what you say, how you look, your abilities and your personality. It will show itself in the way you dress and take care of your physical appearance, in how you talk, in your body language *and* in who you attract into your life.

Whenever you want to change anything within yourself – change your thought process! Put a strong thought in your mind and your actions and your whole being will follow. The chart below illustrates the person we show to the world, based on the thoughts we think.

Old Thoughts	New Thoughts
Blend In	Stand Out
Safe	Self-expressive
Rules	Choices
Quantity	Quality
Trendy	Classic
Following	Questioning
Unsure	Confident

MOVE FROM THOUGHTS TO ACTION

The greatest tool for reality creation is our minds. And enclosed within your mind, are your beliefs, your memories, desires, and your goals and dreams. A negative way of thinking can kill - a loving relationship – can kill your dreams – can kill your hopes – can kill your motivation – can kill your joy – can kill your contentment – can kill your creativity – can kill your financial blessing – can kill your self esteem – can kill a business – can kill your physical health – can kill your mental health.

A person must not only think right – but their personal action must supplement their thought. Faith in yourself, or the lack of it, is the stimulus to attracting all things (good or bad) to you.

Your personal actions must be such that you can rightly receive what you want when it comes to you. A person's way of doing things is a direct result of the way she thinks about things. You can reshape and modify something by simply putting your mind to it. In other words, you can think yourself to the next level and create the life you love.

There are two ways to use your thought process: Scientific and Spiritual. The **scientific** use of thought is to form a clear and distinct mental image of what you want; to hold fast to your purpose to get what you want and to realize with grateful faith that you DO get what you want. Scientists have found that you can become more intelligent based on the more you use and stimulate your brain. Use all of your thinking assets to be where you want to be, doing what you want to do.

The **spiritual** use of thought is to clean out all the garbage from your mind, guard what you see, hear and say and put action behind your faith to get what you want.

Getting your beliefs in order is the key to maximizing your use of spiritual thought. Faulty beliefs can block you from creating the reality you would prefer. Most people don't consider fully the power of their thoughts. The simple, obvious, but often overlooked fact is that the patterns of our thoughts create what's going on in our lives right now.

Every person has the natural and deep-seated power to think what she wants to think, but it takes a lot more effort to do this than it does to think the thoughts that are implied by appearances. Thinking according to what you see is easy.

35

To think something into existence that does not exist, or that you cannot see, is difficult and calls upon the investment of more power than any other labor we are required to perform. It is the hardest work in the world.

YOUR INNER IMAGE = OUTSIDE IMPACT

Your thoughts are powerful. They can pull you under if you allow them, but they can empower you if you manage them properly. This will require doing some 'inner work' – that is, to feed your spirit by relating to and acknowledging the Divine presence within you and allow your thoughts and actions to be directed by the Spirit rather than by external ideals.

Making quiet time for reflection and replenishing will help you become aware of the great strength that lies within you. Then you will begin to realize that your life has a purpose, a destiny, and a meaning that must be discovered. There is a secret wisdom to your inner voice and learning to listen to the voice within is the best way to create a life that is more fulfilling. You cannot look outside of yourself to other people, radio, TV, movies, counselors, psychologists, lawyers or even your circumstances to determine your purpose and a vision for your life.

While you are doing this 'inner work', seeking to discover who you really are, be careful not to look at yourself through 'rose colored glasses', which tends to make everything appear to be covered with a warm rosy glow. If you look at yourself honestly, you are going to discover that there are some things that are going to have to change. major change begins with major introspection. You must identify the enemies of your soul… *low self esteem, procrastination, fear, guilt, pride, arrogance or* (and this is a big one), *past experiences.*

To find the vision you have for your life, you have to look within yourself, where God has placed it. The master key is this – God's will is as close to you as your most persistent thoughts and deepest desires.

A deep personal and ongoing relationship with your Divine self will enlighten your human spirit in knowing who you are and help you to walk in the direction toward what you want.

###

Chapter Two

Becoming Who You Are

*"I believe in the power that not only allows the sun to rise,
but turns seeds into flowers and dreams into realities."*

<u>Oprah Winfrey</u>

---

*B*ernadette stared absentmindedly at her girlfriends on

the dance floor as she slowly nursed her third drink. This one

was going to have to last the rest of the night, because she was

out of money.

Actually, it was already close to midnight and she had

stretched her pocketbook to her 3rd and final drink. "Be

nice to have someone else pay for this kind of thing", she

muttered to herself. It really wasn't supposed to be this way.

She'd left home hours ago with hope and anticipation in her heart that some prince charming would rush to her side, pluck her away from her girlfriends and shower his attentions, affections and drinks on her the rest of the night.

"This routine was getting to be too much of a drag," Bernadette fumed as she watched her girlfriends gyrate their bodies with strangers, licking their lips to send the message that they didn't want to leave that club alone. These men know I'm not a one-night-stand kind of girl, that's why they ignore me", she reasoned.

She would not admit the truth to herself, that the hours of preparation, having her hair done, applying her makeup and changing outfits six times, was solely for the purpose of attracting the man who couldn't keep his eyes and his hands off her ... stranger or not.

*She had left these noisy night clubs feeling unhappy and unfulfilled dozens of times. It was always the same. Throngs of women trying to look uninterested and aloof, while at the same time gyrating in their seats to signal their desire to dance or the desire for a little company. Of course, they'd already have to be drinking so any man that wanted to sample the wares wouldn't have to spend **his** money – that is, until he could find out if it was worth it.*

Bernadette knew she didn't send the 'right' signals in these situations. She also knew that most of the men were of poor quality and probably had another woman waiting for him at home – or sitting alone on the other side of the room. "Why do I keep doing this?" she asked herself angrily.

Bernadette was spending money she didn't have, hoping to attract someone she didn't know, and wasting time doing something that made her feel much worse about herself. She would feel much better taking a luxurious soak in the tub and curling up with a glass of red wine and a good book.

"If you keep doin' what you've been doin' – you gonna keep getting' what you been gettin'!" The words of her Pastor's Sunday sermon rang in her ears as she grabbed her keys and left the club deciding, this would be the last time!

The Real Problem

The real problem was not in Bernadette's situation, but in whom she perceived herself to BE **in** these situations. What appeared to be the **cause** of the problem (no male attention, boredom and the negative environment) was only the **effect** of the real problem (an unsatisfactory self-image and disappointing lifestyle). Of course, once she decided she'd had enough, she had to decide who she was going to BE.

Our lives are a reflection of our conscious and unconscious choices. When we don't choose, we live by default. That which you don't choose will choose you and that which you fear will find you. You choose wisely when you know who you are and how you want to be.

Life does not have to be hard work – it is simply a process of yielding to your Divine spirit for guidance and instruction about what to do, how to think and where you are going.

BE - DO - HAVE

We have somehow come to believe that once we run up on the man of our dreams, lose 50 pounds or come into a lot of money, that we will have arrived and become a bigger and better person. Millions of people look for the perfect diet to follow in order to become thin. They focus on what they have to DO, rather than who they have to BE.

It stands to reason then, that we would look to some wise individual like our pastor or counselor or self-help book that could tell us what we need to DO in order to HAVE what we want. Unfortunately, you and the preacher have the process backwards. When you marry prince charming, or rock that bathing suit or become rich, it will be because of WHO you are, not because of what you HAVE.

So many people go to bars or to work or to their church looking for the perfect person, the person of their dreams. That is what they DO. What they DO is go and look for the 'right person' instead of working on 'being the right person'.

In the creative process, DO-HAVE-BE simply doesn't work, because DO is not the first step in the process of creating what you want. The correct order of creation is BE-DO-HAVE.

Most of us approach life from RIGHT to LEFT. For example, if we want to become something, like married, we often think we need to start by determining what we need to HAVE - - such as beauty, money, a great body, etc. So we try to figure out what we need to DO in order to HAVE those things, thinking that if we DO the right things long enough, we will eventually become married.

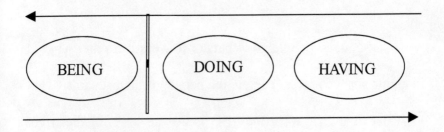

A more powerful approach is to live from LEFT to RIGHT. Start by envisioning yourself as already BEing happily married, then DOing the things that happily married people DO, and you will attract all the things that happily married people HAVE.

The following exercise has three columns labeled BE DO HAVE. <u>Remember to work this exercise from Right to Left.</u> Starting with HAVE, write down everything you want from life that you don't have. Then, in the middle column, state what you would have to DO in order to have what you want. Finally, in the left-hand column, decide who you would **need to BE in order to HAVE what you want.**

BE	DO	HAVE

ARE YOU A LADY-IN-WAITING?

'Ladies in Waiting' are powerless women. Powerless women are those who have given up their personal power that would enable them to live productive lives of poise, polish and purpose; They have too many loose ends that are not tied up; They live in perpetual stagnation; They judge every event and person by the mistakes, disappointments, failures and upsets of the past.

While you don't want to let your past obstruct your future, reflecting on your past serves the purpose of identifying your prior challenges and unproductive patterns.

Sometimes we have to go backward in order to go forward. You have to back out of a driveway before you drive ahead to reach your destination. Considering past events is not a longing for the 'good old days' or a condemnation of how you 'messed up'. This retrospect is done in the context of the present. Its analyzing yesterday not from where you were, but from where you are now, so as not to repeat those unproductive patterns that create problems in your life.

However, there are, so many women who are in love with their own personal drama. When you feel sorry for yourself, that's drama. When you feel guilty or panicky, that's drama. And when you let the past or future conceal your present, you are creating the stuff of which drama is made.

━━━━━━━━━━━━━━

He had told Roberta from the beginning that he did not want to be married. "I would be happy to be your escort from time to time, take you on a trip every now and then

and even come by and mow your lawn when you need me too...

but marriage is not for me!" She of course did not believe him

and was convinced that he would become so enamored with

her sexually that he would change his mind. She'd give him a

couple of years (in fact told him that), and if he didn't propose

marriage after that time frame she was going to move on. That

was six years ago. She's still hanging in there and he's still

uncommitted.

―――――――――

As painful as it is, we must lift the blinds and let the
light of honest self-reflection come in, for change to take place.
And be mindful that this inner work and reflection is not an
excuse to become a 'Lady in Waiting', while you ignore the
unresolved issues you have left behind that can keep you from
going toward your future.

CHECK YOUR BELIEF SYSTEM

We all have hundreds of beliefs that influence the way we conduct our lives. Some beliefs are directly related to our values and feed our spirits, while other beliefs are dated and actually limit our potential. The image of yourself that you embrace comes from your collected beliefs and the judgements you make in regard to what you can and can't do. If your belief system is faulty, meaning that if you have erroneous thinking or misguided notions, you can find yourself 'stuck' or worse, self-sabotaging your life. You see there's what happened to you in your life...and there's what you decided it meant.

Our beliefs are formed from our own personal experiences as well as from information we receive from trusted people in our lives; parents, peers, teachers, mentors and society. Sometimes we struggle through life with beliefs that limit us; then something happens that questions the belief we had, and our world opens up to new beliefs, and possibilities.

Below are some of the limiting beliefs that stop most people from having what they want. If you're honest with yourself, you'll find that you carry many of these beliefs, just as I did. Now tell the truth … do any of these thoughts every cross your mind?

About You:
1. No matter what I do, I should be doing something else.
2. I don't know what I want.
3. Don't get your hopes up too high, you'll get hurt.
4. If I fail, I would be afraid to try again.
5. I should have figured this out by now.

About Money: 1. I must work hard for the money I earn.

2. I need more money than I can generate.

3. I feel overwhelmed in changing my financial picture.

4. Everybody's not meant to be rich.

About Love: 1. I'm not good enough to be loved.

2. I'm not good enough, period.

3. I'm too fat to be loved.

4. I'm too old to be loved.

5. Most men are no good.

6. There are not enough men to go around.

Limiting beliefs can cause you to miss (or not even see) opportunities that are standing in your path. You believe your beliefs to be true, even though you are aware that they are formed based on your *very* limited experiences as one person, in one body, in the entire world.

53

Fill in the Blanks. What are some of your beliefs about the world?

Life is _____

Work is _____

There is _____ enough time

People are _____

Men are _____

Bad things happen because _____

My life is how it is because_____

I am a _____

My body is _____

God is _____

Love is _____

When I make a mistake, I feel _____

Taking a risk is _____

You do have a choice here. You can choose to let go of the beliefs you don't want and you can choose to replace the beliefs with ones that better serve you.

Ask yourself the following. You may write your answers in a journal or just meditate on them quietly here:

1. What do I need to have in my life to feel deeply satisfied?

2. What do I know in my heart is keeping me from feeling satisfied and successful?

3. What situations, relationships, beliefs, attitudes, feelings and choices have I made that are no longer serving me?

Beliefs are how we create reality. Changing your beliefs or conclusions about your past can go a long way toward changing the way you life your life today. In other words, what's going on in your life right now is a result of what you believe. Beliefs are important because they drive our thought patterns and influence our behavior...Think about this for a minute...Imagine if you had a belief that triggered negative thoughts about your intelligence, your appearance, or even the color of your skin...How would those defeating thoughts influence your behavior? Your beliefs set your course. These coupled with your values and decisions are a predictable guide to your future.

HARMONIZE WITH YOUR PICTURE

Forming a clear mental picture of the things you want and holding this picture in your thoughts is the first step toward becoming who you are meant to become. Put this picture with (1) the fixed purpose to get what you want and (2) the unwavering faith that you do get what you want, (3) closing your mind against all that may tend to shake your purpose, dim your vision or quench your faith.

Don't accept bad news or a pessimistic view about anything in your world, from someone outside your world. You cannot retain a true and clear vision of what you are to become if you are constantly turning your attention to opposing pictures, whether they be on the *outside* or imagined on the *inside*. This is where your soul thinking comes into play. The dictionary gives the definition of SOUL as *"the spiritual part of a person credited with the functions of thinking and will, therefore determining all behavior, as well as the emotional nature of a person."* Breaking it down, let's say that your SOUL is the YOU that controls your mind, emotions and your will.

Let go of any negative situations or circumstances that may have adversely affected you in the past. Don't talk about them. Don't cry about them; don't even think of them at all. You give your power away when you dwell in the past. Put unhappiness, loneliness, lack, depression and all things pertaining to what you want eliminated from your life, completely behind you. You see, concentrating on things that are temporary and subject to change, only slows the progress of those things moving out of your life, through your evolution and growth, and blocks what is supposed to be coming into your life right now. You must put your focus on your mental picture of the life you want and who you want to become, to the dismissal of anything or anyone that may tend to dim or obscure the Vision. The truth will set you free and you will know in your gut that you can create what you want to create, you can get what you want to have, and you can become what you want to be.

FOCUS ON YOUR VISION

If you don't know what you want in life, you don't know who you are. Therefore, becoming clear about what you want and don't want from life is by far *the most meaningful journey* you can take on the road to self-discovery. Discovering who you are is a process that results in action and transformation. It is a transformation that brings spiritual enlightenment that will turn your life into one that is productive, purposeful and powerful. When you know who you are, you become clear about what and who belongs in your life...and what and who does not belong there.

So how do you know who you are? You will begin to know who you are by looking at what's going on in your life right now and by recognizing that the situations and circumstances you are experiencing are the result of a previous choice of who you have chosen to BE. Perhaps you have given your PAST most of your power and strength. You can do this by dwelling on it and allowing regret or longing (it goes both ways – no where) to dominate your thought processes. **There are three major things that must be understood in becoming who we are meant to BE:**

Number one, you were made in the Image of God.
This means that you have the presence of God in you,
possessing the same nature as your Creator, with creative
powers you haven't realized or used. Therefore, you have the
power to create your own reality.

**Number two, you are endowed with the ability to
reason and to choose.** This is a reflection of God's intellect
and freedom and also shepherds in wisdom, insight &
understanding beyond what you can figure out by your own
reasoning.

**Number three, there is already a purpose for your
life.** It's your job to discover your purpose. The Master Planner
knows what it is. When you become who you are meant to BE,
you develop a clear understanding of your purpose and path
which is critical to your success. Take quiet-time and go deep

inside your spirit to set a clear, focused vision for your future. This becomes the foundation that drives behavior and brings about your results.

Fulfilling your life's true purpose, which ultimately is self-discovery, requires developing a higher consciousness or of becoming more self aware, enhancing your self-image. Your self- image is the belief you have of yourself, an evaluation of your capabilities and personal worth, which can only be found from within. The real keys for happiness are to: 1) be yourself, 2) like yourself, 3) Discover what you have to give – then give it.

The more you love and respect yourself, the more power you will have. The key purpose in life is **self-discovery**. Know who you are. Many people think that once they know what they want, they know who they are. But it's not until one knows what they have to give that they know who they really are.

Chapter Three

What's Love Got to Do With It!

If I knew all the mysteries of the future and knew everything about everything, **but didn't love others**, what good would I be?

And if I had the gift of faith so that I could speak to a mountain and make it move, **without love I would be no good to anybody.**

If I gave everything I had to the poor and even sacrificed my body, I could boast about it, **but if I didn't love others, I would be of no value whatsoever.**

Love is patient and kind.

Love is not jealous or boastful or proud or rude.

Love does not demand its own way.

Love is not irritable and it keeps no record of when it has been wronged. It is never glad about injustice but rejoices whenever the truth wins out.

Love never gives up, never loses faith, is always hopeful and endures through every circumstance.

1 Corinthians 13: 1-7

Candace noticed Marcus way before he noticed her.

*But she was determined to make sure **that** situation changed*

right away. After 40 minutes of literally following him around

the huge nightclub and placing herself in his path, he finally

looked at her once, and then again. I think it's called a

'double-take'. The tight jeans and low cut sweater she wore

didn't hurt either.

Within two hours they were in bed together, in what was

the beginning of over two years of give and take. It was mostly

***giving** on Candace' part and **taking** on Marcus' part, to the*

tune of two flat screen televisions, unlimited use of her

car, scores of gifts and thousands of dollars...in what she

hoped would buy his love. Candace finally 'got it' when she

came home early from work and found another woman in their

bed.

The Lesson: Love has nothing to do with how much you give up, how much you lose, or what you do. It has everything to do with who you are and who you become.

We throw the word "Soul Mate" around very loosely without unearthing our souls. Your soul is the sum total of your mind, your will and your emotions and this is the KEY.

What's in your soul will set up the circumstances and experiences of your life. The truth is ... the man who takes money and gifts from you without reciprocating with at least a little affection and attention to what you need, is not a GOOD catch. In that same vein - the woman who is desperate and who allows herself to be used and misused and then becomes reliant on him is not a good catch either.

Romantic love is an oxymoron, meaning it cuts both ways. Those women frantic for it are the women who lack it. Those who are unenthusiastic about it are the ones who attract it. What you give to others you also give to yourself. Do you have hidden agendas, unresolved issues, unhealed wounds, or an inferiority complex? When you strengthen your own personal character and become the best you, your relationships will reflect the refined you. Furthermore, it's at this point, that the kind of man you attract will be different.

As a woman, you must learn to accept the fact that in a relationship the main person you are dealing with is YOU.
The love we give to a partner is second-hand. Our first and foremost love is the love we give ourselves. Your partner only reveals yourself to you.

Many women make the mistake of seeing a committed relationship as being the ultimate GOAL, when the real purpose of a relationship is to point you back to yourself in order to bring out your best qualities. Your success at love involves you being accountable for your own destiny – the destiny that God has planned for you.

EXAMINE YOUR 'NEEDS' CHAIN

Each and every one of us has motivations or NEEDS that drive *all* of our life choices. Your personal development must be heightened enough that you can take care of your most basic needs in life yourself, *prior* to 'hooking up' with someone.

Below is the hierarchy or levels of needs that **must** be met in our lives, according to social scientists, beginning with the most basic needs:

1. Survival
2. Security
3. Love
4. Self Esteem
5. Self Expression
6. Spirituality

1. Survival

This is the need for food, clothing and shelter. Regardless of whatever else is going on in your life, your most crucial and basic need is and always will be survival. If there ever occurs a situation in your life where you believe your very survival is threatened, that need will dominate and your choices will show it.

2. Security

The next level of need that can influence your choices is the need to find some basis for physical and emotional security. This is protection from bodily harm and the ability to make a living and take care of yourself. The primary emotional need for everyone is the need for acceptance and belonging, such as the emotional satisfaction that comes from outside approval, or the feeling that you get when you are a part of a couple, a group or organization like your church.

3. Love

Studies of newborn babies reveal that unless they receive love, they will die. As we grow up, if we are not convinced that we possess it, we will go through life trying to find it. Some of our most critical choices have been made for and about and in the name of love.

4. Self Esteem

This means essentially liking who you are and feeling good about your status in life. A person who is described as having "issues" can usually be traced back to a low-level of self-esteem. As a result, you can find yourself making decisions driven by a need to build up how you feel about yourself. Seeking self-validation from others instead of yourself can have an enormous effect on the choices you make.

5. Self Expression

It is extremely important for you to be able to express the gifts that are uniquely yours. When all the previous needs have been met, we may then begin to feel the urge to make a contribution to the world. You may feel the urge to teach, design or create. The need for self-expression is a tremendous inner force that can certainly drive the choices we make for our lives.

6. Spirituality

Choices here are directed by the need to develop a vision for your life and fulfill your goals and dreams. This need requires that you manage your life on a much higher level, which demands a relationship with a power greater than yourself. Try God. As an aside here, these choices are too often **not** the focus of your life if you are dealing with a more immediate need, such as survival.

At what level are you operating right now? According to behavioral scientists, until the most basic need is met you cannot move to the next need level. Therefore, you must be aware of your own needs before choosing a prospective mate.

For example, the lowest needs level is <u>survival and security</u>. If you or your potential mate are dealing with issues like unemployment, divorce, separation, grief and loss, you are at <u>your lowest needs level</u>, struggling for survival and feeling a lack of emotional security and therefore cannot progress to the next level of <u>love</u>.

You must be aware of your own needs before choosing a prospective partner. Now would be a good time to go over the hierarchy of needs list and re-number them according to the level **you** are experiencing now and identify what's most important to you in this season of life. Remember, *if you don't know what you want, you don't know who you are* and also, *if you don't know what you need, you won't get what you want.*

MY CURRENT HEIRACHY OF NEEDS (What's most important to me NOW!)

1. _____

2. _____

3. _____

4. _____

5. _____

6. _____

Completing this exercise will help you 'match up' your needs chain with your potential mate's needs.   Then you can determine what you need from your mate at this time in your life.

Elise had done a lot of hard work in the last three years – mental and emotional and spiritual work...soul stuff.   She knew she wasn't where she wanted to be but she certainly wasn't where she used to be. She had finally reconciled the 'sex thing', didn't

need it and could take it or leave it (thank God) and

didn't feel guilty about it either. Of course, it wasn't

always that way. It used to be that she did whatever –

that is whatever others wanted of her.

Now Elise finally got it! Her significant other had to at

least be as spiritually evolved as she was.

Here is how Elise's **hierarchy of needs** lists shapes up now after doing the necessary 'inner' work:

1. Spirituality

2. Self Expression

3. Self Esteem

4. Love

5. Security

6. Survival

Elise's spirit is what drives her now, which means that she operates on a new and higher level – and she's very aware of the importance of her mate hovering around the same level! It goes without saying that doing the things she enjoys and acknowledging her special talents and gifts was what she was put on earth do.

Eric was a very impressive "catch" on the surface. He was a budding film-maker, former TV talk show host, handsome, a great dresser and was very lavish with his compliments and appreciation for Elise. In fact, he plunked himself right onto her "radar screen" by acknowledging her beauty and femininity, her heightened self- development and her positive sense of self. Then suddenly he seemed to abruptly stop paying any attention to her and grew distant and cold. Elise knew he was dealing with some issues in his life, such as his recent separation and divorce, finding steady income in his chosen field, a new place to live and a dependable automobile.

What she didn't understand was that he was at his lowest level

of the needs chain (survival and security) and therefore unable

to deal with the next level of the needs list, loving and

belonging.

––––––––––––––––––––

The Lesson: Elise does indeed have a dilemma on her hands.

Should she move on to find the mate who was able to

provide the love and belonging she needed or wait for him to

get his survival needs out of the way?

This is the point where many single women drop the

ball and choose the wrong man.   If you are at a point where

you really need to be loved and treated with affection, you

might not want to choose someone who is emotionally

unavailable.

There are some men who have "issues" and they do not deserve a front row seat in your evolved and enlightened life. When you give the **majority** of your time to someone else (this includes your family, your mate *and* your job), you project the message that you are insignificant, that you are of little importance and that you don't deserve very much when it comes to others devoting their time to *you*.

Choose consciously who and what deserves your time and energy. Be your virtuous and genuine self, every day. Decide what you will and will not tolerate in your life. Tolerating disrespect and the lack of what you need from your relationships can wear down your self-esteem.

Let's declare it now! It's time out for emotionally unavailable men! We must learn to reinterpret love, not as a state of anxiety and distress, but as an act of imparting an already enlightened self that rejects the notion of putting up with and settling for a man living on a level below what we deserve.

TAKE THE DRIVER'S SEAT

The biggest mistake in choosing a potential mate is becoming physically and emotionally involved too quickly at a deep level. Humans relate to each other on three levels: spiritual, soul (mind) and body (physical). **Healthy relationships should *always* begin at the spiritual and intellectual levels.**

These are the levels of:

✳ purpose

✳ motivation

✳ interests

✳ dreams and

✳ personality.

The physical level is the least important of the three, yet there is where we usually start! Physical interaction leads quickly to emotional involvement, especially for women. Men seem to have an uncanny way of being able to be physically involved, while leaving their emotions out of it. Thus begins the cycle of allowing our emotions to make all the decisions regarding us and our relationships from thereon.

If the woman who is reading this book gets only one thing from it, it should be this: **You are the engineer and the conductor of your own train!** That means YOU determine the direction, YOU do the driving and YOU decide who can and who cannot come on board.

The main purpose for beginning a dating relationship is to gather information. This helps you determine if you and your potential mate share similar interests and dreams or views on life. Plunging ahead into an emotional entanglement before gathering this information will result in frustrated and unfulfilled life dreams.

When you begin to take over the controls of 'your train' you determine the route you must take to reach your destination. Hopefully you've learned from experience where the forks in the road are, where the hills and valleys are and where the detours are.

Jumping into a relationship before developing boundaries for yourself ... what you will do and will not do ... what you will allow and not allow ... who you are compatible with and with whom you are not, will cause you to relinquish control of your vehicle and enter dangerous territory by default.

"SOMEDAY MY PRINCE WILL COME

There is a fairytale that tells the story of a beautiful princess that lets a frog into her bed and when she awakens the next morning he has turned into a handsome prince. Many women have lofty dreams of whom and what their prince charming should be. They place a lot of confidence in **looking** the part of a woman that can snare the 'right' man by buying expensive clothes, jewelry, shoes and making regular visits to the beauty salon, and I might add...with money they don't' have.

A woman who has ignored her own evolvement and self-development and spends her money on frivolous trappings to impress him in order to be loved, is way below this prince's needs level.

I had a friend once who had very lofty fantasies of what she desired from her prospective mate. He had to be a high-income producer, a home owner and drive a late model, preferably luxury car. He needed to have enough discretionary income to wine and dine her on a regular basis. He had to be someone that shared her love of travel and theater. This meant frequent trips to the Caribbean, Canada and other fun cities like New Orleans and Las Vegas.

She also wanted her man to love the arts, and dreamed of attending plays and shows on Broadway. By most standards, this is a pretty evolved man she was looking for. **Now let's look at what *she* was bringing to the table.**

Her finances were hardly on the level of being discretionary. Oh… she would find the money that allowed her to look well heeled and snazzy at those dinners and plays, but she had no savings. She did live in a nice apartment in a newly gentrified part of town, but she could barely afford to do so. Each rent payment ran into the next because it was always late. In any given month, she would have $300-$500 in overdraft fees levied against her bank account because she constantly spent money that she didn't have in order to make a good impression.

When she went on trips she had to use cash because she was maxed out on her credit cards. Though she'd been to college, she was not well read and informed, so her conversation was pretty basic and boring. At one time, she was very diligent about working out and was quite proud of her body, but her constant worries about money caused her to gain weight, so she more readily offered up her body for sex in order to snare this evolved man she fantasized about.

The Lesson on a previous page applies here:

Many women seek to have a trophy man with all the qualities that can afford her the lifestyle she envisions, but often in reality, her needs level is much lower than that of the man she dreams of.

Real life is not a fairytale. For the sake of love, many women put their self-development on hold, and stifle their needs, wants, feelings, hopes and dreams. They live with the frustration and often suffer disrespect from the man they are seeking to attract, who is far above where they are on the needs chain. Everything this type of woman does is covertly designed to find the man who will adore her and take care of her, while she can barely take care of herself.

Let's face it ladies, if a man is emotionally and spiritually evolved, he simply does not want a woman who will be high-maintenance in the emotional department, who is spoiled and self-centered and who is simply looking to be carried off into the sunset on her "prince's" white horse.

Be thankful that God is providing you the opportunity to evolve into the very best you can be in every area of your life. Then you can move higher up the needs chain and be in a position to claim a mate on the same level. Many women seem to be afraid of their own personal power and fail to realize that they are the love they seek and they are the companionship they desire.

You are the only one who can do what you are looking for someone else to do. Instead of creating a prince charming through self-deception and fantasy, why not totally embrace, acknowledge, support and honor yourself, and therefore create the circumstances you need to make any relationship a good one. It's through good love relationships that we learn the truth about ourselves. We then can attract the experiences, the people, the circumstances and the situations into our lives that help us grow, evolve and move forward.

BEING SINGLE VS. BEING ALONE

Many people have confused singleness with being alone. If one looks in the dictionary under the word single, they would find the following words or synonyms as definition: "separate", "unique", "whole". Unmarried means to be without a spouse, but single means to be all one (alone), a separate, unique and independently whole individual. I will submit to you here, that the reason so many divorces occur today is because people have not learned how to be single!

Know this! If you are not a separate, single and whole person, you really are not ready to be married. Before you can love others, you must love yourself. Not in a self-centered or prideful way, but by discovering who you are and what God has hidden inside of you, a person fearfully and wonderfully made, with an extraordinary dream and vision, an awesome design and incredible abilities.

If you have a healthy self-image, you won't need anyone to become someone. You should take the opportunity while you are single to really get to know God and become intimately familiar with His presence in your life. You may remember when God told Adam, "it is not good for you to be alone", He was dealing with a single, separate, whole and complete human being entirely absorbed with God's purpose and assignment for his life. Therefore, as long as you are *really* single, it is good for you to be alone until you get to a place where you do not need another person to define you or your individuality.

Individuality is important to God – you need to be able to take care of yourself, using your own abilities, gifts and talents. When God can work with a whole person, He can get more done. If you are reading this book, you may be without a man right now. Taking advantage of your singleness will allow God to develop you into a whole, fulfilled, well-balanced and well-adjusted individual. Once you know *whom* you are, *why* you are, *where* you are going and *what* you are to do, *then* and only then are you ready for marriage.

There is a difference between being lonely and being alone (all one). Loneliness is a spiritual disease. This means that your life should be managed on a much higher level. In the beginning, Adam was alone because he was the only one of his kind, but he was completely fulfilled (filled – full) as a person. He had meaningful work to do and he had an intimate and open connection with his Creator. He was completely oblivious to the fact that he didn't have a mate because he never felt the need for a partner.

Become the smart woman who knows the best way to keep a man pursuing you is to keep him fascinated with who you are? Not just with your body, but with YOU! Furthermore, don't be afraid to identify what you are really looking for in a relationship with the opposite sex, such as – devotion to you – understanding – compassion – support and quality time. These are all by-products of love.

Vitality is a secret weapon that dynamic and enchanting women have put to use for centuries. Vitality creates an aphrodisiac undercurrent around a woman. This vitality or aliveness, if genuine, emerges from having inner health, a total psychic wholeness and sense of well being or heightened spirituality. Now when I talk about spirituality, I'm not talking about church attendance. Tapping into your spirit power is about living from the inside out. A quote from a French courtesan in the 17th century observes, "a good woman who has all the qualities of a man is the most wonderful thing in the world." A woman who lives from the inside out emanates an extraordinary feeling of power, an assurance, creativity and a deep desire to grow.

LOVE IS UNCONDITIONAL

God himself pursues a love relationship with you and He is the One who takes the initiative to bring you into this kind of relationship. This relationship, however, is not a one-sided affair. He wants you to love Him back! God doesn't want His women to try to fit Him into their lives, He wants them to place their lives in Him, and develop and nurture an intimate relationship with Him. Experiencing this kind of love relationship with God is His way of preparing us to love another and receive love in return. This becomes a deep relationship that makes your voice familiar to Him and His voice familiar to you. You'll learn to listen to God's whispers, the voice inside your heart, to know what choices to make, what's right or wrong and to discover your destiny.

Love is the most powerful force in the universe and God is trying to teach us how to do it! His love for us is so wide and high and deep we can't grasp it – it surpasses our knowledge!

God's unconditional love will move you out of fear, out of self-imposed limitations, out of the temporary lust of your physical mind and into the unexplored region of your heart. When you recognize the activity of God's unconditional love in your life, you will experience a total transformation in your consciousness and in how you deal with a potential mate.

When YOU allow His love to live in your heart, it's like taking this love and harnessing it into the power you need to love another to the fullest!

###

Chapter Four

The Feminine Mystique

"You are like a private garden, my treasure...you are like a spring that no one else can drink from, a fountain of my own.
You are like a lovely orchard bearing precious fruit, with the rarest of perfumes."

Song of Solomon 4: 12-13

Desiree was definitely in her element as she stood regally in the center of at least five men. There was not a jealous bone in my or my friend Erika's body, as we stood close by. It was a standing joke among us – we loved to hang out with Desiree – because she had "pull"! There wasn't a man within 100 yards who entered her aura that didn't do a take or

94

a double take when he noticed her. And when we were with her, they noticed us too! That was almost 20 years ago, and Desiree still commands the same admiration from not just men, but women too. I'm talking about a woman who has done the work, never shirking the responsibility to herself. She has always been totally committed to personal development and self worth. She works out everyday and runs up to 15 miles a week. She is the owner of her own sales consultant business, so she works from home, which I might add, is a luxury condo overlooking Lake Michigan. While I've never seen her without a date, it seems that for the last couple of years, it has been the same very, very handsome man she's been with. The Grapevine says marriage is on the horizon. Desiree has really got it going on!

WOMAN - A WORK OF ART

The definition of ART is a making or doing of things that display form, beauty or unusual perception. Since we know that woman was God's idea, it becomes evident that He took special care in creating her as a work of art. The scriptures tell us that we are fearfully and wonderfully made and that His workmanship is marvelous. A large part of the *art* of being a woman and the feminine *mystique* depends on how effectively you are able to communicate your unique identity to others.

The Creator gave woman a special anointing – a Divine power, proceeding directly from Him. He put unique qualities in women alone, like *openness, softness, contemplation, nurturing, feeling, receiving, listening, intuition, poise, tranquility, gracefulness, composure, rest* and *wisdom.* These are spiritual attributes. In short, the power you have is internal. It's what is called the *feminine mystique.*

Embracing your femininity has a direct influence of how you affect men. To fail at this is to not only send a message that you don't care about men, but it is also to ignore God's reasons for making women different from men in the first place. To be insufficiently feminine is viewed as a failure in your sexual identity and a failure to sufficiently care for yourself. One of femininity's great joys is in the pursuit of indulgence, which the dictionary defines as gratification of desire or patient attention, (just for the fun of it). At any rate, much pleasure can be derived from these feminine pursuits (shopping, soaking in a tub of bubble bath, manicures, pedicures, makeovers, etc.) as a creative outlet or simply to replenish what life takes out of you. And as an added bonus, the world often smiles kindly on the feminine woman.

The word 'mystique' suggests attitudes and feelings that are unseen or secret, something unexplained and unknown. The way a woman presents herself to the world should carry some mystery with it. As I said in a previous chapter, the smart woman knows that the only way to keep a man coming around is to keep him intrigued with who she really is. In other words, when he can say, "there's something about you..." – that's a wonderful thing.

The *feminine mystique* encompasses another characteristic not listed above, that of *influence*. This is a natural gift God gave to women, which most men either have to learn or buy. Influence is the ability to sway the heart of a man to make him change his mind. For centuries, Eve has been blamed for causing the fall of mankind. But theologians and learned Christians know that God put Adam in charge in the Garden of Eden:

> "... the woman was convinced. The fruit looked so fresh and delicious, and it would make her so wise! So she ate some of the fruit. She also gave some to her husband who was with her. Then he ate it too.[1]"

Eve simply gave the fruit to Adam to eat, without uttering a word ... and he did it! That's influence. This is an invisible power that women should learn to understand and make use of. Possessing this unique quality puts a woman high up on the 'needs chain'. This woman knows who she is, knows what she wants, and knows what to do, and this is attractive to a man.

The mystique woman walks in the poise and polish that is unmatched by those who don't know who they are. Being poised has more than one meaning. In basic terms, poise is the way you carry yourself. It's a favorable impression made that enhances *your* agreeable qualities, the most effective way you communicate your capabilities and how you honor yourself.

The dimension of your poise can project your needs, your personality, your goals and your destination. Your poise can inspire confidence in your abilities and your judgement.

The *mystique* woman treats herself like a million dollars, and the one-of-a-kind irreplaceable original that God created. God wanted you to be perpetually valuable, so he decided to make you permanently rare, like diamonds or gold. Anything that is mass-produced is inexpensive. To find an original piece, one needs a designer. You were born to be distinct, designed by a purposeful God to stand out, not to blend in and refusing to accept anything less than a joyful, peaceful existence. Desiree understood this and enjoyed the fruits of this knowledge her entire life.

THE ESSENCE OF YOU

If you are already, or are seeking to become a *Mystique* woman, you will draw upon your *inner essence*, which is who you are at the core level. This would include your thoughts, feelings, personality and your desires.

Your *inner essence* is infinite, it includes all things. Your *outer essence* would include your physical body and your facial features and characteristics. The *inner essence* and your *outer essence* COMBINED make up the poetry through which you express your soul and therefore releases you to communicate who you are to others. In other words, your image identity is an integration of the inner personality and desires with the physical make-up. Simply put, we are strong, yet we are gentle, we are aggressive, yet we are receptive, we are creative, yet we are nurturing. There is a way to express every mood, feeling and inspiration you ever have as well as expressing your individuality in every situation you find in your life. The key is to always consider WHO you are first, before you consider the self concept you want to express.

INNER ESSENCE	OUTER ESSENCE
Your venerability	Your strength
Your compassion	Your creativity
Your humanity	Your wit
Your sophistication	Your glamour
Your spirituality	Your intelligence

When you learn to combine your outer appearance with your inner spirit, you can exhibit everything you experience through the language of your image identity without forfeiting the special and unique woman that you are. You will begin to feel very excited about yourself...as well as excite those you come in contact with. Irresistible attraction sets in when you have identified and project your essence, and continue to perfect your personal uniqueness. When you make yourself a 'class act' - the best you - all of your connections with others will reflect the empowered and balanced you.

Your image identity is enhanced by appreciating whatever nature has blessed you with, and by understanding exactly who you are, both inside and outside (both your physical body and your spirit). You must embrace these things about yourself as the qualities that make you special and unique and magnify both those inner and outer qualities in the YOU that you present to the world. People are excited to be in the presence of a *mystique* woman.

Though its been said that opposites attract, the truth is that after the initial attraction, being the direct opposite of one's mate tends to *distract* and then eventually repel. In other words, the *mystique* woman will not waste time with someone who does not share her essence or spirit, or who she really is on the inside, deep down.

DEVELOP YOUR PERSONAL STYLE

Your Image is the visible expression of how you feel about yourself and it's an indication of a balanced state of mind. It's the sum of many interconnecting parts: the way you dress, the way you walk, the way you talk, the colors you pick...and even how you deal with others. Personal style is having a sense of knowing who you are and how to express your personality through clothing and actions. When this sense is developed, it becomes a tool that is extremely useful in all aspects of life.

Whatever aspect of yourself you reveal most often is also the aspect, which will become stronger and stronger in your life. Make sure whatever you project through your appearance is the *YOU* that you want to project. Let your image emphasize your strong points and minimize your weak ones.

Good looks depend on a combination of things – good health, a firm body, healthy hair, a sense of style – and most of all, a courageous outlook and approach to life. Courage means taking a step to be someone new. Courage empowers us to take an in-depth, inward examination that leads us to change and enables us to choose a new way to be.

Throw caution to the wind and decide what you would like your image to be:_____ Creative _____ Classy _____ Chic _____Productive _____ Feminine

_____ Authoritative _____ Tailored _____ Wholesome

_____ Sporty _____ Elegant _____ Self Confident

_____ Conservative _____ Upscale _____ Sophisticated

_____ Poised _____ Polished _____Professional.

UPSCALE YOUR IMAGE

#1   **Choose quality over quantity**. The quality of cut, fit and fabric in higher-priced clothing is usually well worth the extra money. Look for natural fabrics like wool, silk or cotton, rather than man-made ones. These fabrics are enduring fabrics with class and clout.

You may never know how wonderful a well-made suit can look until you see it on. Allow yourself the luxury of trying one on. Until you see how a well-cut garment fits you, how it looks, and how it feels, you may not understand the difference it makes. Even though you may not be able to afford it right now, you owe yourself the education of seeing what makes it worth its price tag. At a later date, you may find that same suit or a similar one on sale or at a discount store.

Look at the way it fits your body. Clothes that are made for the mass market must fit tens of thousands of women; the patterns leave enough room for everybody's figure problems. But more expensive clothing is cut for an exclusive few. Feel the fabric. If it feels soft and light, it has what the professionals call "a good hand." Look at the details: the buttons, the pockets, the stitching. Making an individual statement with your clothing implies making an individual statement about yourself. In fact, no matter what you wear, you are saying something about yourself. Let your appearance say who you are: An attractive, empowered woman on your way to the top.

#2 **Avoid the pitfalls of looking too young,** i.e. ponytails, no makeup or even dressing to casually can convey youth.

109

#3   **Leave the dowdiness to your Grandmother.** There are those women who espouse the 'natural look', in hair, makeup and dress. Do not date yourself by wearing the same hairstyle you wore in high school and by not adding any polish to your face *at all.* A little lip-gloss and mascara goes a long way toward adding vitality to your look.

#4   **Keep your hair under control and avoid changing the color too often.** Consistency counts, and monthly changes in hair color shows indecisiveness. Avoid hair bows on the job – they look cute but lack authority.

#5   **Watch those flashy extras.** They make you look overdressed. In the Fashion industry, 'Less is More'. Rhinestones, diamond-studded watches, dangling earrings, and big, bright bracelets and scarves, won't help you professionally.

#6   **Save the Glam for evening**. Avoid wearing super-feminine or frilly clothes on the job. Instead strive for quiet elegance here. Save clingy knits, slit skirts, sheer blouses for after hours.

#7   **Take care of your skin.** All the makeup in the world cannot cover up bad skin. Learn what products to use for your skin type and develop a skin regimen that works for you. A note here about foundation. Foundation is not designed to cover up your flaws, but to enhance what is good about your skin. 75% of African American women have uneven skin tones. The right foundation is simple to provide a flawless finish.

No woman should feel guilty about spending time on herself. Style is not a trivial or silly affair. It's as basic as our human need for self-fulfillment. When we talk about *image*, we don't mean projecting yourself as something that you are not. We all have both favorable and unfavorable characteristics. We can choose the qualities we display and it is not a lie to stress the best.

Believe me, what you really are will show up. The power of intention is very strong and what you really intend to show to the world will come out. Let's consider two women who are about to attend an important social event.

_____

Renee is hoping to meet a man. Wanting to be noticed and desired and sought after, she wears the sexiest, most revealing outfit that she has. However when she gets to the party, she discovers she has exposed more of herself than she wants to and now wants to hide what she's got left that's not showing. Because she feels overly exposed and nervous, she withdraws from connecting with others and may appear to be aloof and unapproachable. Renee may meet the man of her dreams at the party, but he probably won't be interested.

Yolanda, about to attend a swanky dinner at the home of her company's president, has decided to play it safe in a inoffensive evening skirt and plain blouse. As she enters the luxurious living room and the guests glance at her to give her the "first 20 seconds" to make the right impression, she is momentarily inspected and then ignored. Her appearance provokes no curiosity and creates no interest. Feeling the pain of rejection,

Yolanda spends the balance of the evening trying to regain lost ground and begins to move around clumsily, and talking too loudly. In short, she became a self-conscious young woman who was trying too hard. When she dressed that evening, she wanted to portray herself as a confident, efficient, dependable employee, which she was. However she had played up one aspect of herself to the exclusion of other characteristics that were equally important – her charm, her intelligence and her wit.

Both Renee and Yolanda tried for a certain effect. Both failed. If either one had taken the chance of portraying her own personality in the way she presented herself, her evening might have turned out differently. What both women lacked was personal style, a understanding of knowing who they were and how to express their personality through their appearance.

One should strive not to be clothes-conscious or self-conscious, but rather conscious of *self* and how to project her true self in the way she dresses.

Here are some of the messages that the way you carry and 'package' yourself can send:

...you fear success and strengthen your intention to avoid it with drab and boring attire...

...you are setting too safe boundaries on your world and placing barriers in your path.

...you are not ready to pursue new experiences, welcome new pleasures and accept new responsibilities...

Often a woman needs only to make a minor readjustment in the way she looks at herself to effect a major transformation.

POISED, POLISHED AND ON-POINT

Being poised, polished and on-point will allow you to create a balanced and vital existence. Poise has more than one meaning. In basic terms, being poised is the way you carry yourself. It's a favorable impression made that enhances *your* favorable qualities. It's the most effective way you can communicate your ability and the right message about yourself. Your poise can project your needs, your character, your goals, and your life purpose. Your poise can inspire confidence from others in your abilities, self-control and your wisdom, and you can inspire people to want to be around you.

There's a biblical story about a young woman named Esther who had been recruited into the King's palace along with many others, to be chosen as the King's new Queen. Each young woman was required to complete 12 months of prescribed beauty treatments.

"Six months treatments with oil of myrrh followed by six months with perfumes, spices and various cosmetics"[1]

When it was time for each woman to go to the King, she was given whatever she wanted to take with her when she left the harem for the King's quarters. Most of the young women took fabulous jewels and baubles with the hope of adding to her allure. She would arrive in the evening, and in the morning would return to a second harem. She never ever went back to the King unless he took a special liking to her and asked for her by name. When it was Esther's turn to go to the King she asked for nothing to take with her.

117

"Esther, just as she was, won the admiration of everyone who saw her."

Esther was taken to King Xerxes in the royal palace in the 10th month of the 7th year of the King's reign. The king fell in love with Esther instantly - he was totally smitten by her. He placed a royal crown on her head and made her his queen.

The Lesson: The King fell in love with the **real** Esther. When Esther went to visit the King the first time, she was clothed in her own vitality and self-confidence and a highly developed spirit. Esther did not need the artificial trappings of beads and bangles to attract the right man into her life.

CONFIDENCE, THE NEW SEX APPEAL

A confident woman is a self-sufficient woman who belongs to herself. Women who exude self-confidence do not threaten men of quality. By the same token, men of quality have very little interest in women who have no self-confidence. If you find that the man of your dreams seeks to stifle your creativity or acts even slightly envious of your personal power...you're with the wrong man, sister!

Sometimes the unfortunate thing about being raised a traditional woman is that she is taught that the most important thing in her life is <u>security</u> and <u>survival</u>. Many women go through the better part of her life searching for security, or someone to take care of her. Therefore, she sacrifices herself, hoping that if she devotes herself to others, she'll be taken care of in return.

But depending on relationship and life this way often backfires. It also threatens personal development. The wish for this security results in the decrease of assertiveness and self-confidence, for we have been and are still being taught to give up on our dreams and settle for the romantic model.

The irony of it all is that you can't have an authentic relationship if you relinquish who you are, and begin looking at yourself in relation to men. Many women have a tendency to make men extremely fascinating and powerful. They feel they're going to gain access to that power indirectly, even though they actually create his power in their own minds. In the process, their own self-esteem and self-confidence begins to dwindle until they don't have enough 'juice' left to create the kind of life they really want to have.

Making a quality decision about who you really are and the image you want to project will make your self-confidence soar! Maximizing your self-confidence will maximize your sex appeal.

The best way to develop the highest level of self-confidence is to learn to become a little bit more selfish – not self-centered, but to acknowledge your uniqueness and

realize that *you are important!* Release old habits and embrace new ones by mastering these seven (7) steps, and you'll no longer have to worry about *having* self confidence - it just becomes a part of who you are:

1. **Stop comparing yourself to others** - Defining yourself by what someone else does only causes you to tear yourself down if you perceive them as being on a higher level than you are.

2. **Develop personal boundaries** - Stop allowing other people to come into your space to create discord and bring negativity. Anyone that leaves you with a feeling of low self-worth, anger, fear or guilt should be loved for 'afar'!

3. **Forgive yourself when you mess up** - Mistakes are okay - it's the best way to learn important lessons. The most successful people have learned and prospered from their mistakes. The key is to not keep making the same ones again and again.

4. **Eliminate shyness** - I've always thought that people who profess to being shy are truthfully very self-centered. They become overly concerned with how they look to others and thus shut themselves off from the rest of the world.

5. **Learn to 'step out'** - Faith is an action word. Your Creator is very pleased when you have strong faith, trusting in Him, but faith along with your actions makes Him ecstatic and eager to show favor to you in reaching your goals.

6. **Develop a positive self-image** - Whatever aspect of yourself you exhibit most often is also the aspect which will become strong and stronger in your life. Make your image one of polish, purpose and style and your confidence will soar!

7. **Vanquish fear** - Fear will stop you every time. Think of the people you don't approach, the risks you won't take and the decisions you fail to make.

USE YOUR SECRET WEAPON

The *Mystique* woman soon learns that her secret weapon is her spirituality, and the realization that her purpose on earth and her work can be one and the same and that the way to make that happen is guided and directed by her inner spirit. We draw our spirit power from giving and receiving from our unique personality and values...from what's inside us. It comes from listening to our inner voice and placing our lives in the middle of God's activity, so that we find a whole new way of looking at life beginning to unfold for us. You will begin to see that your work and your purpose are not significantly different. It all comes from the same source.

The importance of being spiritually nurtured cannot be expressed enough. What is spirituality? It is NOT getting up on Sunday morning and going to church; It is NOT wearing dresses to your ankles and no make-up; It is NOT crossing your legs on the floor and repeating a mantra for an hour each day. Spirituality is a recreated spirit that allows you to have authority over your reasoning faculties (five senses) and thus ruling your entire being. A person is recreated by receiving God's nature into their spirit, which makes them a New Creation and gives them a new self.[2] In other words, you no longer rely on what you see, feel, and touch, or the circumstances in which you find yourself, but on the

Truth that you understand in your Spirit - you were designed by a purposeful God to NOT fail at *anything* you do.

God has placed an incredible power within you, which constantly responds to your thoughts and words. You have the power and the authority to change your world, by changing your mind. You can learn to control your mind by the conscious choice of thoughts that you have. God's power is

125

always at work within you and is able to carry out His purposes for you. Anything that adversely affects your spiritual life, undermines your emotional health or tends to hurt your testimony (how you present yourself) to the world does not glorify God. You may either place your worth in the status of the man you are associated with, or seek men who fit socially accepted profiles…instead of investing in yourself and striving to reach the heights of your potential.

Developing your spirit means changing your self-concept toward that of perfecting your best talents and your God-given gifts. When you do this, you will begin to feel powerful and attract who and what you want in your life. God has not taken away the strength and beauty He gave you at birth. These gifts are buried within you, covered over by your attitudes and presumptions that prevent you from living the abundant life God has planned for you.[3] This means knowing what you bring to the table and how the table must be set when you get there.

As a woman, you are a miraculous and unique creation with something special to offer. Know that where you are today is a result of your self-concept and what you have chosen to BE.

Your spirit power helps you to perform at peak levels, giving you the grand plan with which to guide your actions and choices. Operating in your spirit power allows you to take full responsibility for your own happiness. A completely responsible woman is attractive to an honorable man who appreciates you for who you are and supports your wants, needs and feelings. Finding and projecting your power is the best way to lure a quality man because it comes from the heart and expresses your true self without deception and paves the way for a deserving man to return your openness and sincerity.

When you are *ready for you,* project the poise and polish that sends the message to others that you have created a balanced and vital existence for yourself.

###

Chapter Five

The Joy of Self-Discovery

"I looked up the road where I was headed, and back the way I done come. And since I wasn't satisfied, I decided to step off the road...and cut me a new path."

Maya Angelou

He really pulled out all the stops that night! The first part of the evening Beverly didn't even pay any attention to him. She wasn't attracted to him that way. She didn't even remember how she happened to be in his apartment. She was, however,

129

very attracted to what she perceived as his fabulous lifestyle.

His apartment stretched a full city block with a 12ᵗʰ floor view

overlooking Chicago's Lake Michigan.

The way he had orchestrated the evening was brilliant!

The Kaluha and Crème flowed lavishly and eventually turned

into white Russians with the addition of vodka. Somehow as

the evening turned into night, what was originally a small

gathering of friends, suddenly turned into just the two of them.

As she prepared to leave, he must have realized her

penchant for partying, and this allowed him to insist on one

last drink in the intimate piano bar downstairs. He never gave

*an inkling that his plans **did not** include him being alone that*

night. There was no enlightened conversation to speak of –

only cold white castle burgers at the bar and more white

*Russians. She had completely lost control of who she **thought***

she was and what she was doing there, some three hours ago.

It was the oldest scenario in the world. Get

astoundingly drunk and end up in bed with a stranger. Beverly

vividly remembered however, some two to three hours later,

him hastily shaking her awake declaring the had an important

meeting and had to leave – and so did she! She barely had time

to dress in the clothes she had worn to work the day before, pat

her hair and rush off to work. He didn't even offer her a

toothbrush.

As he left her on the side walk in front of his luxury

apartment, her dignity in tatters, Beverly realized that it was a

good thing that she'd never see him again.

You've probably heard the old saying, "clothes don't make the man". The Lesson that applies here is that what you see on the outside (luxury apartment) provides absolutely no clues to a person's character, integrity **or** his plan for you! There's a lot to be said for a woman learning how to think like a man does. It's okay to be fascinated by the prospect of having a good time – but it's dumb to be so impressed with what a man chooses to show you, while you lose yourself in the process. This man had a plan from the beginning of the evening – but Beverly didn't realize it – nor did she have one of her own.

The journey toward self-discovery is a spiritual one. It leads you toward defining your purpose and mission in life and inventing or reinventing yourself, if necessary.

Today's woman plays a much more visible role in shaping our world than in the past. And it begins with determining your purpose. Defining your purpose means knowing your passion, and identifying what you enjoy doing... then doing it! However, acknowledging your self-worth comes *before* purpose. Many of us spend our lives suffering from low self-esteem and insecurity because we never come to realize our own self-worth. When all is said and done, making the most of yourself is the *most* significant purpose of all.

Each of us came with a prior design, a blueprint that enables us to make the most of our possibilities. You have been gifted by your Creator with unlimited treasures of ability specifically designed and tailored to accomplish everything your God-given purpose demands. You are equipped with all you need in order to do all you were created to do.

Do you know who you really are? Try the following exercise to know more about yourself and help you answer that question.

WHO AM I? EXERCISE

Use the rating scale on the RIGHT to rate yourself in all areas below.

Rate Yourself From 1 to 10	Ready					Not Ready					Rating Scale	
Healthy	1	2	3	4	5	6	7	8	9	10	Couldn't Be Better	
Self-confident												
Self-love												
Self Worth												
Loving Relationships												
Good Income												
Job Gratification												
Financial Independence												
Time to Enjoy Life												
Spiritually Nurtured												

So, what did you learn about yourself in doing this exercise? Are you ready in some areas and not ready in others? **Start by concentrating on developing those good qualities in which you are deficient.** You will notice that the areas of self worth, self-love, self-confidence are in the top four. Self-confidence is at the top of the list right after your health.

A confident woman is a self-sufficient woman who belongs to herself. The best way to develop the highest level of self-confidence is to learn to be a little bit more selfish – not self-centered, but to acknowledge your uniqueness and realize that you are important. This all begins with developing a assured self-image.

If the majority of your scores were in the 'not ready' column, that is, from #5 to #1 you suffer from some <u>lack</u> in your life. The bottom line is, if you lack anything in your life that would make your life whole and complete if you had it, you are POOR. Now when I say POOR, it has nothing to do with having a good income or enjoying financial independence. The biblical word for 'poverty' is the Greek word 'poucous'. This word doesn't mean you don't *have* anything, it means you aren't *doing* anything.

Wise people say that having what we want from life is quite simple – just choose it. But if life really is that simple, why haven't most of us already chosen to live the life of our dreams?

Actually, there are **several probable reasons** why some have not chosen to have life be that good:

- Who you are *Being* now is blocking that change;

- The quality of living does not fit in with your current reality concept;

- Having your dream come true is outside the limits set by your self-worth;

- You lack the courage and the confidence for choosing outside the box;

- What you want out of life is outside of your comfort zone and *therefore*, so is the development, growth and enlightenment that would allow you to *know who you are* and to have what you want.

It's a hard lesson that anything you want that you don't now have, can only be found outside the box many of us have built around ourselves. Therefore, whatever is missing in your life, acknowledge it now and deal with it!

Unmet needs consume 25 – 90% of life. If you are needy, you attract needy people. The evolved woman has a highly developed sense of self, and therefore sees to it that her personal needs are met because she is oriented around her values. When needs are met, values get clear. Sometimes this woman affects others so profoundly that she often unconsciously helps others discover who they are and what they have to share with the world.

A major purpose of experiencing conflict is for self-discovery. Asking yourself the question, "who am I really", on a regular basis, will at least give you a leg up when the time for a new change comes around. And you'll find if you keep on living that the self-image and identity you have of yourself will constantly need to be redefined.

CONQUER THE ENEMIES WITHIN

Personal fulfillment can only be attained when the numerous levels and elements of ourselves are satisfied. This means that we can evolve into our extraordinary potential by overcoming your negative self-perceptions and self-imposed limitations.

There are three things that break us and keep us from having all that we want from life.

(1) **Procrastination**: Putting off decisions and actions until a later time or never deciding anything when a decision is in order, wastes your ability and TIME, which is

God's gift to us and our most valuable asset. When you spend your time trying to find out what's best for you – you're doing just that – spending your time. How valuable is time? Time properly <u>invested </u>is worth a fortune. Time <u>wasted</u> can be total destruction, so invest your time. Indecision robs you of opportunity and undertaking. The secret to winning is action!

(2) **Mental laziness:** This is the line of least resistance in keeping you from reaching your goals. The YOU that is in you is the YOU the world is looking for. Forming the habit of concentration, strategizing and downright hard thinking is vital to you having complete control over your life. Listlessness is a dangerous enemy. "Ho-hum, forget about it, I'll just drift along". But guess what, you can't drift yourself to the top of the mountain.

(3) **Wrong talking, and Negative thinking:** Most of us are like an old neighborhood – undeveloped. It shows signs of beauty and significance, but it is covered up by dilapidated buildings and decaying yards and sidewalks that need to be rehabbed, landscaped and replenished to make its

141

real beauty shine through. The way you think plays a large part in what you say, and what you say often determines the actions that you take.

Recognizing and doing battle with these enemies will propel you toward the development of the fertile resources within you as well as build up your courage to fight what's holding you back. Consistent and repeated acts of courage are required in your pursuit of what you want and the person you want to become. And, this starts with turning on your POWER.

TUNE INTO YOUR TRANSFORMATION

It is a fascinating fact of life, that almost everyone on this planet wants the quality of their life changed in some way, but almost no one wants to be transformed. And you can't have one without the other. Having what you want from life can't happen any other way. To have that quality-of-life change, you must first raise your level of thinking and grow some in consciousness.

The change from being who **you are** to who you need **to be** is executed in a spiritual way. I'm talking about the creative flow, the new ideas, the inward spiritual power by which you can do all that you want or need to do.

Begin to see how wonderful God made you! We are meant to be whole in every area of our lives – spiritually, emotionally, physically and mentally. However, this will require:

143

- being able to forget our past mistakes

- seeing the present as transitional and to focus on the future.

Living in the gifts and callings that God has given you requires living out a_life of faith. Faith in yourself is the pipeline through which your power flows and the size of that pipeline sets the boundaries of what you can have in life. By the same token, your potential power could be *restricted* by your own lack of faith in yourself, for you will only be as powerful or as powerless as you perceive yourself to be.

It's a universal law that if you keep doing what you've been doing – you're going to keep getting what you've been getting. One of the things that most women need to acknowledge and change is the self-limiting habits we have. These are habits that *we* create, not our Creator. The way you now use your mind is a habit, and habits are nothing but repetition of our own thoughts. Therefore, we have the capacity to change them.

Repeated patterns show us what our needs are. For every habit we have, for every experience we go through over and over, for every pattern we repeat, there is *a need within us* for it. We must be willing to release the need we have for whatever is holding us back. When you take a good honest look at yourself, analyze what you see, and don't be afraid to change anything you see that you don't like. Most people don't change because they don't see their own faults. They don't

145

realize that their beliefs, attitudes and patterns have played a major part in who they have come to BE.

Never be afraid to make the effort to get better – to change. A person is old only when they refuse to change. The unavoidable truth about life is "change, or you will be changed". Gone are the days of just operating in the status quo. Sometimes it becomes necessary to redefine ourselves and change will do that. For this reason alone, transition can be frightening, especially if you have defined yourself by what you *do* rather than by who you *are*.

When thinking about transformation, it might help to remember that you've been "being transformed" all your life. Since the day you were born, you've been growing in consciousness, becoming more aware of who you are, finding your personal power, choosing who you will be. All your life, you've been being reborn by renewing your mind.

Even so, most of us will see transformation as a fearful thing -- something to be avoided at all costs, because being transformed takes us outside our comfort zone. And that's a little scary to think about. But it's also true that the only place you'll ever come to know who you really are is when you've found the courage to venture outside of that zone.

Transformation happens in three different ways:

1. **The gradual transformation...** So gradual, that you wouldn't notice your growth, any more than you'd notice that your hair has grown some since the last time you looked in the mirror.

2. **The forced transformation...** Like having your father die and being forced to take over the family business, or like losing your job, It's any abrupt happening that forces you to grow and become the one who can handle this new problem you're facing.

3. **The intentional transformation...** That's when you decide you don't like the way your life is going right now and have made up your mind to change it.

Let's assume this is your current situation -- that you want that prosperous new life, but fear the unknown outside your uncomfortable but safe reality.

Transformation is truly the key that unlocks the door to your new reality

So, the question becomes, how badly do you want your circumstances to change? And are you willing to give up your current mind-set in order to have what you want? If you're seeing transformation as overwhelming, I assure you that being transformed requires no more than a change in the pattern of your thinking. It's simply, a *renewing of your mind.* And if changing your mind -- (acquiring a different mind-set) -- would give you the life you want, wouldn't it be worth it, no matter what you had to pay to get it?

Transformation takes focus. King Solomon gave this wise advice in the Book of Proverbs, "Look straight ahead, and fix your eyes on what lies before you. Mark out a straight path for your feet, then stick to the path and stay safe. Don't get

149

sidetracked." Another translation for this last sentence is "Turn not to the right hand nor to the left." This is what "focus" is all about.

There will be people, places and things that will try to take you off your path of change, because they fear change themselves. I have found that when situations and circumstances begin to significantly change in my life, or even when I start to experience a certain amount of unrest with my current reality, it's a sign that God wants me to make a new move. It's at this point where you will need to listen for the still, small voice of God and move when he says move. You must learn to say "so long" to those issues that threaten to leave you immobile and use your God-given faith to step up and out.

In every endeavor you must live with faith in the power of your right thinking, the potency of the words you speak and the purposefulness of your actions. Above all, you must know in your heart of hearts that having the 'God kind of faith', which creates oceans and moves mountains, is the key to living fuller, richer, more meaningful lives, all the time.

The woman who gets the life and the man she wants, has to "get with the program". She must work hard to be the best that she can be at whatever she does. We often have to talk ourselves into or be literally forced to make a move through certain situations or circumstances – but move we must. The <u>Transformed</u> woman knows that indecisiveness will kill any type of fulfillment she seeks out of life and that she can't take forever to decide which way she wants to go either. Just like "ole man river", life just keeps rolling along and time will run out.

TIME – A God-given resource – is a commodity that can neither be bought or sold. The only thing you can do with TIME is to use it. If you don't use it, you lose it. The only TIME you have is NOW, so get busy and use it wisely.

Decide to use every minute of your day constructively, effectively and efficiently. You will begin to learn to use your time wisely, by examining how you spend it and who you invest it in. Let's face it, it takes courage to be someone new.

Having courage means resisting your emotional feelings, and mastering the fear (not the absence of fear).

Once you begin the process of self-discovery, it becomes key to eliminate those people from your life that come to steal your time. You'll need it to get where you're going.

QUESTIONS TO THINK ABOUT – EVEN IF YOU DON'T PHYSICALLY ANSWER:

1. If you won the lottery and never had to work another day in your life, what things would you want to accomplish?

_____

_____

_____

_____

2. If you were told you had six months to live, how would you

   spend your time?

   _____

   _____

   _____

   _____

3. At the end of your life, what would you most like to be

   known for?

   _____

   _____

   _____

   _____

4. What reoccurring interest have you had since you were a

   child?

   _____

   _____

   _____

   _____

   _____

5. Identify Your Passion

   _____

   _____

   _____

   _____

   _____

6. What are you truly knowledgeable about

_____

_____

_____

_____

_____

_____.

7 SIGNS OF SELF-SABOTAGING BEHAVIORS

Sign #1   FOCUSING ON WHAT IS NOT
              WORKING OR NOT RIGHT.

Problem: Finding that you think a lot and speak a lot

about what is going wrong can make you feel

dissatisfied and can subdue your sense of purpose and

ambition. Notice how often you speak about things that

aren't working.

Sign #2   BEING STUCK IN FEAR.

Problem: Do you worry a lot about the future and

what is going to happen or might happen? Are you

thinking about your fears so much that you are

paralyzed and take no action because of fear of what

might occur?

Sign #3   FEELING YOU HAVE NO VALUE

Problem: Do you forget all your accomplishments and lack pride in who you are and what you have accomplished? If you stew and obsess about the past or your lack of success or lack of goal achievement, then you'll be stuck in noticing how much you lack as a person. If you often criticize yourself or can't accept compliments, you aren't allowing yourself to love yourself.

Sign #4   COMPARISON OF SELF TO OTHERS.

Problem: Do you constantly compare yourself to others and then feel badly when compared to them? Comparison doesn't motivate us to do more or be better, instead it makes us feel we'll never be good enough and we aren't right now.

Sign #5   MEETING GOALS AND THEN
LOSING THEM.

Problem: Do you not believe that you deserve to accomplish goals and that you are entitled to what you want? What is the story underneath – maybe that you aren't good enough to have it?

Sign #6   CHASING AWAY RELATIONSHIPS.

Problem: Do you always feel something is missing in your relationships or find fault with the other person? Perhaps you are afraid of intimacy. Underneath this is usually a fear of abandonment or exposure that causes you to distance yourself from others.

Sign #7   HAVING NO PURPOSE.

Problem: Do you feel you have no reason for being? No purpose in life? We all have some purpose for being on the planet and it is time to notice yours.

Comfort Zone

I used to have a Comfort Zone Where I knew I couldn't fail

The same four walls of busy work were really more like jail.

I longed so much to do the things I'd never done before,

But I stayed inside my Comfort Zone and paced the same old floor.

I said it didn't matter, That I wasn't doing much

I said I didn't care for things like diamonds, furs and such

I claimed to be so busy with the things inside my zone,

But deep inside I longed for something special of my own.

I couldn't let my life go by, Just watching others win.

I held my breath and stepped outside and let the change begin.

I took a step and with new strength I'd never felt before,

I kissed my Comfort Zone "goodbye" And closed and locked the door.

If you are in a Comfort Zone, afraid to venture out,

Remember that all winners were at one time filled with doubt.

A step or two and words of praise, Can make your dreams come true.

Greet your future with a smile, Success is there for you!

Author Unknown

Chapter Six

Create the Life you Really Want?

"You get what you want, not what you ask for"

Barbara Stanny, author
"Secrets of Six-Figure Women"

The moment one definitely commits oneself then Providence moves too. All sorts of things occur to help one that would never otherwise have occurred...

Johann Wolfgang von Goethe

It took Lauren four cities, six different jobs and three marriages to realize she had to change her way of not only doing what she was doing, but also change the way she was thinking. Her lack of self-worth caused her to blindly accept what was presented to her from every man she married, which was acute jealousy, coupled with absolutely no desire for personal growth. They also lacked entirely the concept of being in any kind of 'partnership'. It was the same with her career. She constantly over-compensated for her lack of formal education (even though she was always successful at what she set out to do), by putting in long hours and tolerated being overlooked for raises and promotions. It wasn't until years later, when she finally got fed up with being taken for granted, and being an under earner in her 'chosen field', that she realized she had been taking the 'safe' route all her life – thereby working at jobs where she knew she couldn't fail. After all she reasoned, "who wouldn't be a successful typist after 20 years of typing for someone else?

She decided to "grow some courage" and take a chance on herself, do the inner-work necessary to think BIGGER, and employ the dynamic qualities that God had placed in her.

———————————————

Now would be a good time to take inventory of the circumstances, environmental factors and relationship unhappiness you have in your life that you could do without. Spend some time with yourself and gather up the little pieces of yourself you have given away and ask yourself the following questions:

1.   What kinds of people do I allow in my life?

There is an axiom that says, "we attract who we are." If the people in your life or those who are *trying* to come into your life cause you to feel inadequate, unloved, unworthy or insignificant and leave you with an overall feeling of discouragement, it could be that deep down inside this is how you really see yourself.

2. How do I feel about the relationships in my life right now?

This includes your relationship with your money, your work and with people as well. Of course, this question is a no-brainer if you have everything you want, such as a fabulous lifestyle with lots of money and a handsome 'significant other'. Though if that were the case, you wouldn't be reading this book.

3. What do I want my lifestyle to BE?

There are those that say the best way to know what we want from life is to realize what we *don't* want. That may be true for <u>the first step.</u> But we should then take it to <u>step two</u>, by replacing the 'don't want' lament with a focus on just the opposite of what we are dealing with. In other words, instead of saying "I don't want these bills" and focusing on that – say, "I have more than enough money to take care of all my desires".

Knowing what you don't want is simply your current reality. And that can change. When you have given yourself the power to say NO to what you don't want, you are on the road to having what you do want.

The Bible tells a story about the potter and his lump of clay and the steps he takes to create a pot. When a potter works on a pot and sees that it has a defect in it, the potter either re-molds the clay and begins again or if the pot already has been baked in an oven, the potter has to smash it and start over. You may need to use this same process to begin creating the life you want.

WATCH THE DREAM KILLERS

The two most powerful dream killers are your **past** and **fear.** We've already acknowledged that F.E.A.R. is actually *False Evidence Appearing Real.* Letting your past serve as evidence of your self-concept and self worth is shooting yourself in the foot. This cripples your spirit power coming out of the gate. Tapping into your spirit power enables you to conquer the fear that can create hindrances to the development and maturity that can hinder your realizing your dream. This lack of personal development dictates what you do in life and neglecting to face your fears causes you to relinquish the power God has placed in you. When you allow everything you dream, think, say and do to be controlled by your Spirit, your physical senses (what you see, taste, hear and feel) will no longer control your activities and personal development.

SEEK THE POWER OF INTENTION

The dictionary defines intent as being firmly directed or fixed; earnest, intense; strongly resolved; having the mind or intention firmly directed; stretching out; one's mental attitude including purpose, will and *determination.* Intention is a power that is present everywhere as a field of activity. This intention vibrates through you towards your potential for a purposeful life. Intention = results, always. This is a basic truth about life.

The power of intention is the power to expand and increase all aspects of your life: spiritual, personal, family, vocational, social, and financial.

1. **spiritual** – intend to spend more time doing something for others, such as volunteering; spend

more time in prayer and meditation; decide to find a church home if you don't have one, and if you do have one, join the choir or the usher board or an out-reach ministry.

2. **Personal** – Join a gym or fitness center and start a regular exercise program; take a trip to some place you've always wanted to go; Go back to school or take a certification course.

3. **Family** – Cook dinner for your not-so-immediate family members (aunts, uncles, cousins); pick a regular day each month to spend with your son or daughter (separately) or if you have no children, with a sibling or elderly relative; help with a

relative's education; take a child in your family on a vacation with you to an 'educational' destination, such as our Nation's Capital, the Grand Canyon or Africa.

4. **Vocational** – Decide you're going to be promoted within the next 12 months; Take on a special project at work without being asked; Start your own business.

5. **Social** – Invite a friend to dinner this week; Join a club or reading group to make new friends and develop new interests.

6. **Financial** – Start tithing at your church or to your favorite ministry; Start saving to purchase a new car or a home; Get completely out of credit card debt within the next two years.

Your sub-conscious mind is very, very powerful. It is the last line of defense in the process of resisting change. It experiences reality through the senses, organizes the thought processes rationally and governs all your actions. Look closely and you will see that what you've gotten from life so far is what you intended.

The one thing that is usually misunderstood here is that your *willpower is not nearly as powerful as your imagination.* Just try to picture yourself doing something that your imagination doesn't want to do. Your imagination allows you the marvelous indulgence of *thinking from the end.* There is no stopping anyone who thinks *from the end* - because you can use the components of the All-Creative Source to make it happen.

One of the tricks of the sub-conscious mind is to pretend to go along with what you say you intended – when it really has a different intention and controls what you actually get. Therefore when you think you have committed to a new way of life and it isn't transpiring, take a long hard look at the results you are getting – it is what you intended.

WISE WOMEN WIN

Wisdom is the ability to use knowledge to benefit us in all that we do. And where does this ability come from? Most of us who have studied these matters are aware of the limitations of *sense knowledge*, recognizing that we are spiritual as well as mental and physical beings. It takes wisdom to understand the limitations of depending on what you see, hear, taste and feel to rule your life. Spiritual things are as real as material things, therefore we should plan on spiritual things just as we do on material things.

The Five senses have been the tutors of the brain. This is the only method the brain has of acquiring knowledge. Scientists have discovered that the brain has no creative capacity or ability. It can comprehend the messages of the senses, correlate and categorize them. In other words, it can organize this knowledge so it can and will be utilized to advantage.

The mind cannot invent. It can experiment as in chemistry, but it cannot develop anything that the senses have not bought into it. The most astonishing thing discovered, however, is that *the brain cannot provide wisdom*. The five senses cannot provide wisdom.

Your character is shaped by wisdom and understanding. What about your decision making capabilities? Everything that you are today is the result of the decisions you have made Do you allow your emotions (fear, doubt, anger) to make your decisions for you? Are you continually making the same mistakes or even find yourself in the same place, doing the same things, fighting the same devil year after year?

It's never a good idea to make a permanent decision about a temporary situation and this is absolutely the wrong time in your life to make bad choices.

Why women need wisdom:

1. To identify the unsupervised areas of your life.

2. To make the right choices for life, family and career

3. To become a woman of substance

4. To sustain you and cause you to get better and better

5. To get what you *really* want out of life.

Most do not realize that when God created them, He did so in His own image and likeness and that their spirit is actually the real person. When you allow God to recreate your human spirit by transmitting His own nature into it, you will have God's nature, ability and His wisdom. Your recreated spirit must then take charge and start to dictate to the reasoning ability. Wisdom will help you to expose the shadowy areas of your life *and* the unsupervised areas of your life.

> *"I live a life guided by wisdom – therefore I won't limp or stumble as I run."*   Proverbs 4:12

You must decide the conclusion of your life that you desire. You must pursue the relationships that matter to you. The quality of the relationships you have chosen mirrors and exposes what matters the most to you. Love those who love you more and devote yourself less to those who don't. Sometime you have to hang on to someone else's belief until yours kicks in. But by all means, don't allow those who benefit from your time and efforts to stop you from reaching your Divine destiny. This is how wise women win!

YOU ARE CO-CREATOR WITH GOD

Realize that when God created you, He did so in His own image and likeness and that your spirit is actually the real person. When you allow God to recreate your human spirit (become born again) by transmitting His own nature into it, you will have God's nature, ability and His wisdom. Your recreated spirit must then take charge and start to dictate to the reasoning ability.

You are co-creating your own life. Your life isn't happening without you. Don't let anything stunt your spiritual growth and keep you from expanding the vision of yourself and discovering the meaning of your life. It is your responsibility to make use of the qualities that God has gifted you with, surrendering your dream to the power greater than yourself.

When God wants to birth something great in your life, it will usually be when you are in a season of your life that you may perceive as loneliness.

I've found that these are the times when God wants me to be alone. Why? So He can reveal His presence, His purpose, His plan and His power. Isolation will induce complete dependence on His Spirit, who provides direction and instruction to us.

I believe God uses this period for us to develop a co-dependence to having Him in our lives. Many of us make the mistake, during these times of isolation to search for substitutes for the emptiness and loneliness we feel. This is when a lot of women get into trouble. They will throw away all semblance of pride and relentlessly pursue the wrong man at the wrong time for the wrong reasons. The most important thing you can do during your moments of solitude is to pursue God. He is waiting to give you information you need for your life's journey.

Therefore, in the process of creating what you want, if you become what you think about, and what you think about is getting what you want, then you'll always be wanting. So the key is to reframe the question - *How do I go about getting what I intend to create?* The answer is this. We are all made in the image of God. This means that you can do what God can do...Create. Become just like the all-creative Source (Intention/God) and you will co-create all that you have in your mind.

Once you recognize the presence of Spirit operating in your life, it is at this point that you will encounter one of life's most difficult challenges – that of telling yourself the truth! You will need to look at yourself truthfully, acknowledging and accepting what you see. When you do this, you may find that some aspects of you require attention. Some need a small amount of work, others may even need intensive care. How you feel about you is the foundation of how you experience the world.

Your level of self-esteem influences every choice you make and how you view the world and your place in it. Acknowledge your doubts and fears, your weaknesses and your bad habits, then allow your Spirit to guide you. Discover what and who is in your life that you don't want and what diverts you away from your purpose. Holding yourself in high esteem is your greatest priority.

You must know the real truth about you, that **you are uniquely gifted, exquisite as you are and designed to achieve whatever you want out of life.** There is great wealth buried within you, allow yourself to develop the art of being a real woman and live and love life to the maximum!

Living a full life should become your mantra. A full life includes boosting your income in a way that fits who you are, making the best use of your time and being decisive about what is really important, and cultivating relationships in your life that help you to grow.

Why not expand your view of who you are and what you deserve, to the point that there will be no limit to what you can achieve. If you allow your evolution process to be controlled by the One who created you in the first place, you will be on the road to creating the life you want. And, *when you are ready for you*, you will project the poise and polish that sends the message to others that you have created a balanced and vital existence for yourself.

> *"Whatever you can do or dream you can, begin it.*
> *Boldness has genius, power and magic in it."*
> *-Goethe*

###

You Are The One You're Looking For

Chapter Seven

Maximum Impact – Ascending from Ordinary to Extraordinary

Extraordinary *(extra-or-di-nary)*, **adj.** *1. Out of the usual order or custom 2. Going far beyond the ordinary degree, limit, etc.; very unusual; exceptional; remarkable*

Marcia was at the top of her game where it concerned her career. A former investigative reporter for a big city newspaper, she knew all the right questions to ask and had the innate ability to put the answers together in a cohesive and creative way for anyone to understand. And being in that line of work, there was nothing she hadn't seen or observed about every day life. She later became vice president of marketing for a Fortune 100 corporation. However, she seemed to become catatonic when it came to her personal life. She was constantly left at the proverbial door of one-night stands - never quite able to be or show her true self to the men she came in contact with.

She didn't seem to have any answers as to why she was so unlucky in love. Her education and career-savvy were of no help to her when it came to attracting men. If fact there was almost a self-sabotaging element to Marcia. She was an attractive woman under the surface, but she went out of her way to be just the opposite. Though she was petite in statue, with a nice figure, she wore unattractive clothes and it was obvious that her clothing dollars went elsewhere.

*She had long, thick flowing hair (it was all here's too), which she often wore unkempt and seemed to seldom wash. The neighborhood she lived in was trendy, but she had rented furniture throughout her entire apartment, which was as unkempt as her appearance. Even though Marcia met many quality, unattached men along her career path, the unresolved issues of an absent father and an abusive mother took its toll on her throughout her entire life. She was a classic example of a person who placed little value on herself. She never learned a universal truth - **that you have to consider yourself more valuable than what you can buy, or you will sell yourself short.***

Many women make mistakes about their life's priorities in their image that is both damaging and needless.

Generally speaking, when a woman does not dress up to her potential, it's not necessarily due to a lack of class, but often to a misguided sense of who she is and what she wants to tell the world.

Why not set yourself apart and be a different kind of woman?

The chart below describes the difference between being ordinary and extraordinary.

ORDINARY	EXTRAORDINARY
Blend In	Stand Out
Playing it Safe	Self Expressive
Obeying the Rules	Making Choices
Quantity	Quality
Trendy	Tasteful
Following	Questioning
Unsure	Confident

Our Creator never intended for us to be normal. In fact He calls those who believe, *peculiar people*. This is made clear by the fact that out of the 6 billion people on this planet, no two people are alike. Your fingerprints, the irises in your eyes, your chromosomes and your DNA are distinct and unique. You were designed to be uncommon, special, irreplaceable and rare.

In actuality all people were created to be originals, just like Him and thus, it was meant for us to live extraordinary lives.

DO YOU NEED AN IMAGE OVERHAUL?

IMAGE...the one you project--- symbolizes a healthy state of mind. Your outward appearance should express your level of purity, love, beauty and spiritual joy. How you present yourself to the world also expresses your level of creativity, courage, honesty, faith, wisdom and personal power. Your Image is the visible expression of how you feel about yourself and the direction in which you are headed, and plays a big part in attracting the mate who shares your disposition and your destination.

Your projected image is the sum of many interconnecting parts: the way you dress, the way you walk, the way you talk, the colors you pick...and even how you deal with others. Are you serious about living a successful life, personally and professionally? If the answer is yes, then

191

realize one thing: Your abilities and talents alone are not sufficient. It is the *Image you project* that gets you noticed by those that take you seriously. Your outward appearance provides identity clues, and an unspoken visual code that expresses not only your talents, abilities and personality, but also your needs and desires. It shows who you are and *what you want.*

A negative self-concept expresses your level of despair, discouragement, anger and loneliness, and shows up in your outward appearance and actions, causing you to appear to be unfocused, unfulfilled, bitter and/or Insecure. Allowing these feelings to overtake you will create in you a heavy, burdened and failing spirit and indicate a lack of poise in how you present yourself. It will also cause you to attract a man of the same ilk.

If you're looking for a man of quality, the worst thing you can do is portray yourself as a desperate, lonely and unfulfilled woman! He will back away from you causing your self-image to plummet even further.

Ever wonder why he doesn't call when he says he will? Or why he acts interested one day and uninterested the next? It's because you are projecting the wrong image!

What do you have to offer the man you're attempting to attract? I'm not talking about material things or outward beauty. I'm talking about your spirit. Men want to be around women who are intriguing and confident. Are you really ready to 'go for' what you want out of life? Does your image project that?

Today's woman must elevate the way she views herself and treats herself. You must see yourself as God sees

you, not only through what you do, but also in your thoughts, feelings and desires.

God gave you beauty when He made you. He wants you to look and act like he made you to be. Fashionable clothes, cosmetics and the latest hairstyles are great, as long as you know in your heart why you are choosing to look like you do:

-   Are you covering up feelings of insecurity and loneliness by dressing provocatively?

-   Does loneliness and despair cause you to have an uncaring, dreary look about your appearance.

- Does lack of a general feeling of well being, good health, or enough sleep, show up in a disheveled and thrown together look? Or, and this is the kicker,
- Are you using your physical appearance (face, body, and clothing) to attract the opposite sex?

MAXIMIZE YOUR GAME

Being the best at what you do without settling for mediocrity is the easiest way to maximize your impact. It's a sad fact that many women will never discover who she really is. She will not make the worthy decision to maximize every element of her life by completely using her gifts, talents, abilities and capabilities, and step away from the ordinary to the extraordinary.

It's been said that the richest place on earth is the cemetery. It's filled with the wealth of potential people have taken to the grave with them.

It is essential that each of us ask ourselves the following questions:

- Have I become all I am capable of?

- Have I stretched myself to the maximum?

- Have I done the best I can do?

- Have I used my gifts, talents and abilities to their greatest extent?

And ask yourself this too – is there something missing in my life? Could it be an unrealized dream or an unrecognized purpose?

Being able to answer these questions will allow you to fulfill your God-given destiny, seize your purpose for life, develop and cultivate your skills, expanding your knowledge and maximize your impact on your community and the world.

YOU'RE A DESIGNER ORIGINAL – UNIQUE AND SPECIAL

You are a designer original, a masterpiece designed by an awesome creative power. God knows what is in you because He put it there, distinct characteristics and your very own uniqueness. This means you are rare.

- Diamonds are expensive because there are no two alike.
- Gold is costly because it is difficult to find.
- The Mona Lisa, painted by Leonardo DA Vinci in 1513 is considered priceless and inestimable and therefore uninsurable.

Let's examine what being UNIQUE really means? It means Original never having occurred or existed before; it means Authentic – being genuine or real; it means Firsthand – From the original producer or source; it means Un-copied and Unprecedented – nothing has preceded it, or it's unheard of. YOU are all these things!

You have a high value placed on you and no one else on earth has been designed to do what you were created to do. The woman was made with worth, dignity, expertise and purpose. Your Creator has special plans for you if you would just be who you were created you be.

THE ATTRACTION PRINCIPLE

Attraction is a skill set that you can develop which will attract the best people, ideas and opportunities to you.

Attraction is success without striving. To orient around attraction, you must become selfish (not self-centered), but realize you are important and become attractive to yourself.

Get a fulfilling life, not just an impressive lifestyle. This means basing your life on internals and not externals, and requires a total commitment to personal self-development.

93 percent of what we communicate is non-verbal. **When people meet you, they base 55% of their initial impression on what you look like, 38% on what you sound like and just 7% on what you're actually saying.** This means that talk is not only cheap, but also practically of no-account when it comes to making an impression. Without uttering a single word, you reveal a great deal about yourself,

you goals and your destinations. The unspoken messages you transmit through your body language attitude and attire, strongly affect how others perceive you; you could be sabotaging your life success by sending the wrong message. In this country, fifty-five percent of what we believe about one another – whether or not a person is well educated, intelligent, competent, important, and prosperous – is based on our observation and interpretation of *non-verbal* signals.

That old saying, "beauty is in the eye of the beholder," means the one that's doing the looking is the one that's doing the judging. Have you ever noticed that you experience better treatment when your look is pulled together? And we all know what it's like to be treated badly when we sell ourselves short with a shoddy appearance.

Clothing Messages: Your clothing message relates to the world your talents, your needs, your personality, your moods *and* your destinations. Some people don't have very positive feelings about themselves and these negative feelings come through in the way they dress. If you feel disapproving about yourself, and have doubts about your appearance and your abilities, or if just looking in the mirror is a painful experience – its time to rethink what your clothing is saying about you. Your clothing says, "I feel beautiful", or "I'm important", "I'm successful, "I feel great", or clothes may reveal, "I don't have very much confidence in myself", "I'm depressed, or "I'm angry.

Body Language: Your smile and your handshake are your first contacts with a client or associate. A genuine smile implies sincerity and honesty - convey that message with your smile

202

and you've got the upper hand before anything has even been said. Your handshake also influences other people's impressions of you and says a lot about your self-image.

A firm, confident handshake will convey a high level of self-esteem, while a non-assertive person can reflect her feelings in a weak handshake. Shake hands with <u>directness, firmness and conviction</u>. Accompany it with direct eye contact and a smile!

There are 3 steps to maximizing the Attraction Principle in your life:

1. Seek God – The Universe – Your Higher Power - and ask for guidance in achieving what you want from life, so that it's reflected in your persona.

2. Visualize and Feel your desire. This means having what you want and making it resonate, acknowledging the actual *feeling* of having what you want.

3. Allow what you want to get to you. Put up a 'force field' of sorts against every negative thought or belief. Find a way to move the resistance in your mind out of the way.

YOUR PERSONAL VALUE SYSTEM

A major study done at Harvard some years ago unveiled the **eight** decisions that are made about a person in the first 20 seconds of meeting, with no verbal communication whatsoever.

These are decisions about:

1. Your Economics 2. Your Social Background 3. Your Education 4. Your Economic Heritage 5. Your Trustworthiness 6. Your Home Training 7. Your Successfulness and, 8. Your Moral Character.

All of these characteristics orient around your **personal value system.** In short, what drives you and where do you stand in the game of life?

- Your values provide the framework within which you live your life and also help you make difficult decisions.

- Values are not attitudes, but are principles by which attitudes are created.

- Values are not behavior traits or personality, they are ethical standards that control personal effectiveness and the impact you have upon your world.

What do you stand for? What do you believe in without compromise? What are the things you will do and will not do to have what you want in life?

Does your life reflect your values? This is everything that is important to you or special about you. The little things you love make you who you are – special and different from anyone else.

Identifying your values enables you to also know your identity, your uniqueness and your potential – which are all tied to your purpose.

Explore your values:

1. What do I love?

_____

_____

_____

2. What do I really enjoy?

_____

_____

_____

3. What do I believe?

_____

_____

_____

Below are the most frequently suggested values as defined by our society:

__ Achievement __ Compassion __Courage __Creativity

__Faith __Health __ Honesty __ Independence

__ Knowledge __ Loyalty __ Morality __Physical Appearance

__ Pleasure __ Power __ Recognition

__ Responsibility __ Self-determination __ Self-discipline

__Wealth __ Wisdom __ Work.

Now, put a number in front of each value in the order of their importance to you. For example, the values of Wisdom, Faith, Health & Self-discipline are my top four and were numbered 1-4 respectively. A note here, your top three or four are your *core (or basic)* values.

After these are selected, go ahead and number the rest from the most important to the least. It's important to realize that each higher-order value will take priority over the lower-order values, so if your order is wealth, health and honesty, you will sacrifice your health and honesty for achieving wealth.

YOUR PERSONAL MISSION STATEMENT

(A roadmap for the unfolding of your life)

It is important to strive for a distinct perception of where God is taking you and how to get there. Successful corporations always keep their **Mission** before them and so does a successful person. A Mission Statement:

- describes your unique purpose in life.

- It captures what qualities you want to develop,

- what you want to accomplish, and

- what contributions you want to make.

A personal Mission Statement becomes a guide for your life. Inspiring you to make the decisions that will best help you reach your goals and fulfill your vision.

A Mission Statement is:

- a hand written or typed out paragraph

- posted some place you can see it regularly

- committed to memory

- has specific, measurable outcomes

- has a deadline one-year from today

Here's a process you can use right now to create a Mission Statement for personal success in your career or business and your life in general. Grab a pen and paper:

Step A. Write down 5 positive personality characteristics you like about yourself in your career/business or general work life. For example: <u>willingness to learn</u>, <u>persistence</u>, <u>creativity</u>, <u>friendliness</u>, <u>intelligence</u>, etc.

Step B. For the items you listed above, describe the

way you express each positive characteristic on a regular basis in your career, using the word "by" to begin each phrase. For example, if you listed "willingness to learn" above, you might write "by being committed to ongoing professional development" right next to that characteristic. Another example: if you wrote "persistence" above, you might write "by making sure the job always gets done" below.

Step C. NOTE: Any specific financial goals should be listed separate from these 5 goals.

Step D. Look back over Steps A, B and C, circling the 3 most important items in each column.

Step E. Now fill in the blanks of the following paragraph:

My MISSION is:

_____

_____

_____

_____

_____BY_____

When finished, you will have a short paragraph that reads something like:

> *"My mission is to express my intelligence, creativity and people skills by continually learning and applying new ideas, by finding unique solutions to my clients' problems and by building a powerful network of contacts, a steady flow of referral and renewal business, full technological competence, and at least $125,000 in gross commissions by this date one year from today."*

TIP… Write ideas for your mission statement; Describe how you want to live and who you want to be.

TAKE YOUR TIME! You may have to start over several times, but it's worth it! I encourage you to follow the guidelines above of posting it where you can review it, committing it to memory and reciting it daily. Then you won't need to make any more fruitless resolutions -- you'll have a MISSION!

The **ordinary** woman is influenced by her environment. The **extraordinary** woman develops the self-discipline and spiritual focus to shape her own life. She can rely on a well-developed Spirit to help navigate her life and manage her environment as well as the quality of the people and resources that influences all of us.

###

Epilogue

We must raise ourselves to the level of Energy
where we are the light we seek, where we are
the happiness we desire, where we are the love
we feel is missing, where we are the unlimited
abundance we crave.

Dr. Wayne Dyer, Author
The Power of Intention

Hopefully, if you've reached this part of this book you have learned and will begin to (1) identify your gifts and purpose, (2) focus on who you *really* are, (3) take the driver's seat in your life, (4) Use your secret weapon, (5) realize the joy of self discovery to (6)   create the life you really want and (7) ascend from an ordinary woman to an extraordinary one.

Woman, find the perfection in yourself!   In short, YOU ARE THE ONE YOU'RE LOOKING FOR.

###

Made in the USA
Charleston, SC
20 April 2010